WORKPLACE MORALITY: BEHAVIORAL ETHICS IN ORGANIZATIONS

WORKPLACE MORALITY: BEHAVIORAL ETHICS IN ORGANIZATIONS

BY

MUEL KAPTEIN

*Partner at the Auditing, Advisory and
Tax Firm — KPMG and Professor at
Erasmus University Rotterdam,
The Netherlands*

United Kingdom • North America • Japan
India • Malaysia • China

Emerald Group Publishing Limited
Howard House, Wagon Lane, Bingley BD16 1WA, UK

First edition 2013

Copyright © 2013 Emerald Group Publishing Limited

Reprints and permission service
Contact: permissions@emeraldinsight.com

British Library Cataloguing in Publication Data
A catalogue record for this book is available from the British Library

ISBN: 978-1-78350-162-5
Originally published in Dutch by Business Contact publishers, Amsterdam, 2011.

ISOQAR certified
Management System,
awarded to Emerald
for adherence to
Environmental
standard
ISO 14001:2004.

Certificate Number 1985
ISO 14001

INVESTOR IN PEOPLE

Contents

Introduction

Why do even the most honest and conscientious employees sometimes go off the rails?

What pushes upstanding and intelligent managers over the edge?

What causes benevolent organizations to lead their customers, employees, and shareholders up the garden path?

These questions of the twists and turns of right and wrong in the workplace are intriguing, frightening, and more timely than ever.

First these questions are *intriguing*. How do trusted people and organizations become cheats? Not just once, but repeatedly and systematically. What motivates and possesses them? What explains these twists and turns? How come factory workers went so far as to regularly bind a colleague naked to a push cart and push it through the production room as a joke to lighten the mood? How did a manager, having skirted around environmental regulations year after year to the benefit of his employer, eventually reach a point where he was able to boast about it? How did a director come to pay a customer under the table, by way of friendly service, and still tell the tale dry-eyed? What led teachers to the point that they announced with pride that they had boosted their students' grades so that they could graduate quicker? And what inspired Jeffrey Skilling, president of American energy company Enron, bankrupted in 2001 because of the biggest case of accounting fraud in history at the time, to say shortly before its downfall: "We are doing something special. Magical. It isn't a job — it is a mission. We are changing the world. We are doing God's work." They did indeed change the world, as it is partly due to this fraud case that the Sarbanes–Oxley Act was introduced, an act which had implications for the governance of companies worldwide.

These observations on the behavior of "good" people, however, are also *frightening*. If they unconsciously and unintentionally do wrong, then you and I might also dupe others without knowing it, overlook important matters, and miss the point entirely. This is scary because it means that when we think we are doing the right thing the opposite might be the case.

In spite of our good intentions, things may go wrong and we might even be forced to pack up and leave. Take, for example, the senior executive, celebrated one day and maligned the next, after it became known that he had been selling substandard products for years, in the genuine belief that he was offering customers a good deal. And what to think of the vendor who always made a big turnover, but was arrested after it became apparent that he had been fixing prices with the competition for years. He truly thought that this was normal and to the benefit of the economy. Then we have the chief financial officer who always achieved good financial figures, but had to pack his bags when it turned out he had been fiddling the books for years. He had actually been under the impression that creative bookkeeping was part and parcel of his organization's mores.

Unfortunately these questions regarding the behavior of people and organizations are *more timely than ever*. The recent financial and economic crisis has exposed the human factor in the inner workings of organizations as never before. Society thought it had organizations well in hand, with the Sarbanes—Oxley Act and various other legislation and governance codes, but fencing organizations in with procedures, systems, and structures provides no guarantee that people will do the right thing. Indeed, it may well make matters worse (as we will see later in this book). Since the crisis, regulators have paid considerably closer attention to human behavior within organizations and what causes this behavior. Fields of study dealing with behavior within organizations, such as behavioral risk management, behavioral compliance, behavioral sustainability, behavioral auditing, and behavioral business ethics, have all been booming ever since. Organizations also pay more attention to behavior by investing in cultural programs, professional development, codes of conduct, and soft controls. The question underlying all these efforts and activities is what the explanations are for the behavior of people in organizations, and how we can use this knowledge and insight to protect ourselves and others from future disasters.

This Book

For all those who work in or for organizations and for anyone dependent on them, it is essential to know what explains the good and bad behavior of people within those organizations. If we can explain this, we are better placed to judge, predict, and influence both our own behavior and that of others. Social psychology offers a wealth of answers to the question of why people do bad things, some of them very surprising, thereby explaining the way in which social mechanisms influence the psyche and thereby people's behavior. This book therefore examines the reasons people succeed or fail at staying on track from the perspective of social psychology.

The book draws on both classic and recent experiments. In each chapter at least one experiment will be discussed. Although there is always something artificial about experiments, they offer the advantage that, with all other factors kept constant, the relation between a limited number of factors can be studied in detail. Both laboratory experiments and field experiments come under review, and are applied to current developments, issues and challenges.

This book consists of 52 short chapters in total, each of which can be read individually, but which also complement one another. The first eight chapters lay the foundation for examining the behavior of organizations and individuals. This introductory section discusses matters such as people's moral nature and how their environment influences their behavior.

The remaining chapters are organized according to seven factors which influence people's behavior within organizations. I discovered these factors in the course of my doctoral research, when I analyzed 150 different derailments within organizations. Since then, these factors have been tested in various studies. In a recently published article in an international journal I show, on the basis of a survey of managers and employees, that the more prominent these factors are, the less unethical behavior takes place at work. The factors are as follows:

1. *Clarity* for directors, managers, and employees as to what constitutes desirable and undesirable behavior: the clearer the expectations, the better people know what they must do and the more likely they are to do it.
2. *Role-modeling* among administrators, management, or immediate supervisors: the better the examples given in an organization, the better people behave, while the worse the example, the worse the behavior.
3. *Achievability* of goals, tasks, and responsibilities set: the better equipped people in an organization are, the better they are able to do what is expected of them.
4. *Commitment* on the part of directors, managers, and employees in the organization: the more the organization treats its people with respect and involves them in the organization, the more these people will try to serve the interests of the organization.
5. *Transparency* of behavior: the better people observe their own and others' behavior, and its effects, the more they take this into account and the better they are able to control and adjust their behavior to the expectations of others.

6. *Openness* to discussion of viewpoints, emotions, dilemmas, and transgressions: the more room people within the organization have to talk about moral issues, the more they do this, and the more they learn from one another.
7. *Enforcement* of behavior, such as appreciation or even reward for desirable behavior, sanctioning of undesirable behavior and the extent to which people learn from mistakes, near misses, incidents, and accidents: the better the enforcement, the more people tend toward what will be rewarded and avoid what will be punished.

Finally, in Chapter 52 an experiment is presented which explains how people deal with ethical dilemmas by means of a combination of the above factors.

The factors are not discussed exhaustively. The experiments discussed are, however, selected so as to illustrate important points in relation to the factors listed, and more importantly, are looked at from a different perspective, so that in reading this book you will gain a broad view of the significance of these factors for your own behavior, the behavior of others, and the behavior of organizations. The parts of the book which address the factors are not all of equal size, because some factors are more complex than others, and some factors have been the subject of more interesting experiments.

Enough introduction, let us begin on what I hope will be a morally stimulating journey.

The Context

The following eight chapters lay the foundation which enables us to better examine the behavior of organizations and individuals. We discuss the moral nature of people and the influence of the environment on their behavior. We shall see that concepts such as "right" and "wrong" are present from an early age and that the environment plays a significant role. This knowledge forms the foundation for examining in the rest of the book how organizations influence people's behavior and how we can use this for good.

Chapter 1 discusses the fundamental question of the extent to which people are good or bad by nature. Chapter 2 shows that the goodness of people depends on the price one is prepared to pay for it. The question is then not so much whether a person is honest, but rather in what situation and to what extent. There is also the question of whether people are better able to resist big or small temptations. Chapter 3 shows that this is a nuanced issue. Chapter 4 then addresses the question of the extent to which people are helpful and altruistic by nature, and thereby do good, even when it conflicts with their own interests.

How we see people affects the way we treat them. Chapter 5 is about how we can set up a "self-fulfilling prophecy": whether people do right or wrong depends in part on how we see them. Chapter 6 looks at the way in which our image of ourselves affects our own behavior and asks to what extent people are capable of self-knowledge. In Chapter 7 it will become clear that we have our own prejudices, which distort our perspective and raise all kinds of problems. Chapter 8 finally examines the extent to which people's environment influences their behavior. Here a distinction is made between "situational" and "systematic" influences.

1 Good or Bad by Nature? Empathy and Sympathy

"We must stop seeing the people behind the counter as criminals." These are not the words of a prison director or police chief. They are the words of a chairman of a big bank, and at a significant moment too: at the low point of the financial crisis in 2009. "It's time we started trusting our employees and clients."

What was up with this chairman? Had he completely lost the plot? Had he been living on another planet? Had the crisis not just exposed the fact that people are egotistical, and only out for themselves? Bankers had sold defective products on a grand scale to maximize their own bonuses. This was the quintessential white-collar crime, the greatest in history, according to the film *Plunder: The Crime of Our Time*. And according to United States president Barack Obama the cause of the crisis was "excessive greed," which had been completely unjustified. Had this chairman understood nothing of the words of the American president?

In explaining and influencing people's behavior, we must first address a fundamental question: How do we regard "people?" If the management of an organization see their employees and customers as criminals, then strict measures must be taken to keep them in check. Their freedom of action is restricted and supervision and control are intensified. The company quickly becomes a prison, with the management seeing themselves as the guards. The outside world, however, is bound to view the situation differently, seeing the directors as top criminals, and is therefore particularly keen to restrict their power.

As long as science has existed people have debated whether humankind is good or evil, and whether this is a matter of nature, or comes from upbringing, education and environment: the nature—nurture debate. Classical economic theories would have us believe that man is egotistical, and focused on satisfying his own needs. If we can choose, for example, between two products of the same quality, then we choose the product with the lowest price, because this is to our advantage. According to the English philosopher Thomas Hobbes (1588–1679), people are wolves: the bestial nature of man means that we are purely focused on our own interest. We are heedless of others and competitive to the core. We only behave socially and cooperatively out of a sense of self-preservation. Without the intervention of a higher authority there would be permanent war.

At the opposite end of the spectrum from Hobbes was the French philosopher Jean-Jacques Rousseau (1712–1778). Rousseau was of the opinion that people have a preference for good: "Man is by nature good and happy; it is society which destroys original happiness." According to Rousseau it is the corrupting influence of the environment, of society, which incites man to do wrong and therefore makes him unhappy.

The question as to who is right is not an easy one. Research by Kiley Hamlin and colleagues gives us a hint at the answer. They were interested in the question of the extent to which people are naturally able to distinguish right and wrong. Only if people can make this distinction can they determine whether they want to behave accordingly. In order to establish this, research was carried out among young children, because they are not yet fully formed.

In the study babies aged six months had a large wooden board placed before them. To the left on the board was a picture of a mountain. A wooden figure with two big round eyes then moved toward the mountain. The figure was controlled by the researchers on the other side of the board, out of sight of the baby. The figure tried to climb the mountain, but fell down when it reached half way. This happened again on a second attempt. When the figure climbed the mountain for the third time, another figure was added: the helper or hinderer. The helper also came from the right and pushed the figure to the top. The hinderer came from the left, from the top of the mountain, and pushed the figure down, so that it failed to reach the top for a third time.

Both figures were then placed in front of the babies on a tray. The researchers were curious as to which figure the babies would pick up. Would it be the hinderer or the helper? And what happened? In all cases the babies picked up the helper and left the hinderer. Even when the researchers varied the colors and shapes of the helper and hinderer, the results were the same.

According to the researchers this is evidence that people are capable of distinguishing right and wrong from a very early age, even before they can speak. We are able to determine what is good and what is harmful for others. Evidently we possess empathy from a young age. But not only that: we also have a tendency to choose the good. However limited the experiment may have been, and however primitive the distinction here between good and evil, this suggests we feel sympathy for what is good.

This positive observation is an important starting point for the rest of the book. If people feel empathy by nature, then that helps us to determine how we should set up organizations and how we can best do business and work together. It is then not just a question of imposing and enforcing (the so-called "compliance approach" of rules, controls and sanctions) but also, or even primarily, of cultivating what is already present in the seed (the so-called "integrity approach" of virtues, reflection, and appreciation).

Was the chairman of the bank quoted at the start of this chapter a wolf in sheep's clothing? Did he pull the wool over everyone's eyes in pleading for management on the basis of trust? The research of Hamlin and colleagues does not provide support for this. What we can suppose is that he had not lost his childlike, positive view of the world.

2 What Is My Price? Integrity as Supply and Demand

The book started on a positive note, and that's lucky, as we have some terrible examples to get through. The fact that people can tell right from wrong from a young age, and also have a preference for right, does not mean that they always do right. Wrong can sometimes be very attractive.

Before becoming president of the United States, Abraham Lincoln (1809–1865) was a respected lawyer in Illinois. One day a criminal came to him. "I would like to ask you to defend me," said the man. Lincoln, who had a sneaking suspicion of the kind of person he was dealing with, replied with the question: "Are you guilty?" "Of course I'm guilty. That's why I want to hire you; to get me free." "If you admit guilt to me," Lincoln explained, "then I can't defend you." The man reacted with amazement: "But you don't understand. I'm offering you a thousand dollars for your services!" Although a thousand dollars was a large sum of money at the time, Lincoln resolutely refused. The criminal replied, "Mr. Lincoln, I'll offer you two thousand dollars if you defend me!" Again Lincoln refused. In desperation, the criminal played his trump card: "Mr. Lincoln, you're the best lawyer in the area. I can't have travelled all this way for nothing. I'll give you four thousand dollars." At that moment Lincoln flew from his seat, grabbed the man by his collar, dragged him out of the office and threw him into the street. When the man had stood up and pulled his clothes straight, he asked Lincoln: "Why did you throw me out when I offered four thousand dollars? Why not for one or two thousand, or when I admitted guilt in the first place?" Lincoln replied: "You were nearing my price!"

Apparently Lincoln's integrity had a price: he was "for sale." For a certain price he was prepared to throw his principles overboard. The question is whether everyone has a price. In order to answer this question, as in the previous chapter, we should perhaps start by exploring our innate qualities.

Michael Lewis and colleagues researched the extent to which people have an innate ability to resist temptation. For this purpose he took children of three and five years of age as his subjects. Each time a child was led into a room and asked to go and sit at the table. The researcher then walked behind the child's back to set up a large toy. He asked the child not to look around. They would be allowed to see the toy later. Having set up the toy, the researcher said that he needed to leave for a moment. On leaving he asked the child again not to look around. The child was now alone in the room and was exposed to the temptation of looking around. After a maximum of 5 minutes the researcher came back and asked the child whether he or she had looked.

38 percent of the three-year-olds said they had looked, even though this was not the agreement; quite a letdown. Lewis had, however, filmed the children when the researcher left the room. What did he discover? The footage showed indisputably that almost all the three-years-olds had looked. Only 10 percent had not. It turns out that most of the children who claimed not to have looked behind them were lying. Half of the children had therefore not only broken the agreement, but had also subsequently lied about it. What about the five-year-olds? They all denied looking behind them, while two-thirds had actually done so. So over time lying increases, though fortunately it seems so does the ability to resist temptation.

According to Lewis, lying begins with learning to speak. Of course the offense of looking around in the experiment and lying about it is pretty innocent in the scheme of things. No one was put at a disadvantage by it. It does, however, show that most people are unable to resist temptation by nature and that lying starts at an early age.

Lewis incidentally found that children with a high IQ lied more often. That does not bode well if it is people with a high IQ who hold positions of responsibility later in life. All the more so, since temptations also increase. At work there are countless temptations. It is quite a challenge to keep on the straight and narrow when major interests are at stake: that sorely needed contract that can only be won with a backhander, that fall in the share price that can only be avoided by slightly distorting the figures in the annual report, that mass lay-off that can only be prevented by temporarily skirting around environmental law, or the fiercely desired promotion that can only be achieved by sabotaging the other candidate.

The good thing about Lincoln was that he did not allow himself to be bribed. He knew his price and acted accordingly. When we know the price, which is established according to supply and demand, we can work out which situations we must avoid in order not to fall prey to temptation. If money burns a hole in your pocket, it would be wise not to take on a financial role. A reckless person would do best to avoid becoming a risk manager. Those with a tendency to lash out would do better to avoid stressful jobs. These are important matters. Because the same goes for both the economic market and the market of integrity: sold out is sold out.

The question is not so much whether people are honest, as how long and under what conditions, what temptations they can resist, and at what point they relinquish their integrity. As William Shakespeare put it, "For who so firm that cannot be seduced?" Everybody has a price; the question is what that price is. Lincoln knew his price. Do you know yours? How much can you be bought for? And what is the price of people you depend on, or for whom you are responsible? How "price-elastic" are they?

3 Bagels at Work: Honesty and Dishonesty

Many company canteens are currently experimenting with self-service check-out systems. The classic situation forces employees, after selecting their meal, to pass a cashier before sitting down to eat. But a cashier costs money, and for that reason many businesses have converted to another system: employees must use a self-checkout system, without the involvement of a cashier. Some supermarket chains are also experimenting with this. Can people cope with the responsibility? In this case no large sums of money are involved, such as those that Lincoln was exposed to in the previous chapter.

The story of the "bagel man," described by Steven Levitt and Stephen Dubner, is very enlightening. Out of the blue they received a call from a certain Paul Feldman offering his sales figures. Who was Paul Feldman, what did he sell and what did he have to show them?

Paul Feldman had worked for the Center for Naval Analyses in Washington since the 1960s. He had acquired the habit of buying bagels for everyone whenever his department won a new research contract. Because this proved popular with his colleagues, Feldman decided to bring some in every Friday. This quickly became a success, also attracting colleagues from other departments. Eventually Feldman was taking fifteen boxes of bagels to his office every week. To cover the costs he placed a money box with the price next to the bagels.

In the 1980s, when new management took over, Feldman decided to leave and make selling bagels his profession. He went around offices in Washington with a simple proposition. Every morning he would put down one or more trays of bagels by the entrance to the canteen, and beside it a wooden box with a slot in which consumers could put money. It turned out to be a gap in the market. Within a few years he was supplying 8,400 bagels to 140 offices.

Because Feldman kept track of how much he picked up from each company, he collected interesting data and a fine experiment was created: stealing was simple, so the only thing that counted was the integrity of the consumer. In his old department takings were 95 percent. Everyone knew Feldman, so why wouldn't they pay? Feldman therefore blames the remaining 5 percent on carelessness on the part of his colleagues. But what was the yield when he made this his profession? When he began it was 91 percent, and that fell gradually over 20 years to 87 percent, although there was a 2 percent recovery after the 9/11 terrorist attacks. Only one money box was stolen each year.

The facts of the bagel man case show that, when it comes to paying for a bagel, most people act honestly. Clearly many people, once they have reached adulthood, are able to resist this small temptation. Nonetheless, one in seven people abuses the opportunity and does not pay.

It is therefore naïve to assume that everyone is always honest, even in small matters. Pinching a little piece of the pie, bending a rule once in a while, occasionally telling a white lie, just looking the other way for a moment, that's all it takes. Some companies that had decided to get rid of cashiers in their restaurants therefore changed their minds. Initially the payment behavior remained the same and in some cases even increased, but after a while standards dropped so low that the losses were greater than the cost of the cashiers. The trusted cashiers have therefore reestablished their place in these companies.

But are they really trusted? Research by Thomas Gabor and colleagues shows that cashiers too are only human. Researchers visited a shop as a customer, bought a newspaper for 30 cents, paid the cashier with a dollar bill, and walked slowly out of the shop, seemingly absent-mindedly, without waiting for the change. There was plenty of time for the cashier to call the customer back and give them their change. Still 16 percent did not, which incidentally fits in nicely with Paul Feldman's figures. Another study shows that in more than three-fifths of cases not giving change results from carelessness or sloppiness on the part of the cashiers, and in the other cases from dishonesty.

All this raises the question whether people are more prone to be dishonest when it comes to petty misdemeanors, odds and ends (where both the misdemeanor and the gain are small), or when it comes to serious transgressions (where both the damage and its fruits are significant). Is it easier to resist small or large temptations? Little research has been carried out in this area. An exception is research by Ephraim Yuchtman-Yaar and Giora Rahav. They had bus drivers in Israel give back too much change to passengers and varied the amounts involved. They found that the more change was given back, and therefore the greater the temptation for the passenger, the more female passengers kept the money and the more male passengers gave it back. For men, as the temptation increased, so did the sense of responsibility, whereas with women the opposite was the case, according to the researchers.

Petty misdemeanors in organizations should not be trivialized. The workplace is full of small temptations like Feldman's bagels. Figures show that, whether it's stationery (especially at the start of the school year), toilet paper, or milk and sugar sachets (especially at the start of the summer vacation), employees take them in large quantities for private purposes without permission. And the slightly larger crumbs are also almost daily fare. KPMG research among the American working population shows that over a year, 21 percent witnessed a colleague overclaiming expenses, 18 percent saw a coworker stealing property belonging to the organization, and 15 percent were aware of unauthorized business gifts being accepted within the organization.

When a chairman was presented with such figures regarding the situation in his own organization, he waved this away with the words: "There are big, general sins, the deadly sins, and there are daily, petty sins. We're talking about the latter here. This is *peanuts*." But perhaps values lie precisely in those petty matters. Watch the pennies and the dollars will take care of themselves. It's the small things that matter. The criminal often begins as a petty thief. *Penny wise, pound foolish* is a criticism often directed at organizations. The opposite can be equally dangerous, however, as when the owner of a discredited construction company once said, "An entrepreneur should think big and act small. You stumble over the threshold, not the fence."

4 Egoism versus Altruism: The Theory of the Warm Glow and the Helping Hand

The previous chapters addressed the issue of honesty at work (the experiment with the bagels) and the extent to which people have an innate appreciation of helpfulness (the experiment with the moving figures on the wooden board). But *valuing* helpfulness is not the same as *being* helpful, helping another when needed, even when you don't get anything out of it or it comes at a cost. Does altruism really exist?

According to Abraham Lincoln, who makes his second and last appearance in this book here, pure altruism does not exist. One day Lincoln was riding in a coach, in heated discussion with a fellow passenger on the question as to whether helping another is really altruistic. Lincoln argued that helping can always be traced back to one's own interests, whereas the fellow passenger maintained that there is such a thing as true altruism. Suddenly the men were interrupted by the squeal of a pig trying to rescue her piglets from drowning. Lincoln ordered the coach to stop, jumped out, ran to the stream, grabbed the piglets, and set them safely on the bank. Back in the coach his fellow passenger said, "Well now, Abe, where's the selfishness in this incident?" "The reason for my action is a good question," Lincoln replied. "That was the very essence of selfishness. I should have no peace of mind all day had I gone and left that suffering old sow worrying over those pigs. I did it for my own peace of mind. Do you understand?"

According to Lincoln, self-interest always plays a role, even when we help others. Pure altruism does not exist, only enlightened self-interest. We help one another in order to achieve peace of mind, to soothe our consciences, or to feel good about ourselves. In the literature this is called the "warm glow theory." Economist James Andreoni came up with this term at the end of the 1980s in relation to philanthropy to emphasize, more than was thought at the time, the importance of internal motives for donating to good causes. People give money to a good cause not only to support that cause, but also because of the glow they get from the idea of being helpful. People help others to become better themselves, even if "becoming better" is purely a warm fuzzy feeling. All kinds of studies support this hypothesis: people who help others feel better, happier, and healthier. In fact, the reverse is also the case: people who feel good are more willing to help others.

But there is more than just calculating altruism. People are spontaneously altruistic by nature. Felix Warneken and Michael Tomasello have shown this to be the case. Their experiment focused on toddlers of 1.5 years. They were confronted with different scenarios in which an unknown adult, the male researcher, had difficulty achieving a goal. The adult accidentally dropped a felt-tip pen on the floor but could not reach to pick it up, and tried and failed to open a cupboard door with his hands full. For every scenario there was a control in which the adult had no difficulty, for instance intentionally throwing the pen on the floor.

Each experiment consisted of three phases: for the first 10 seconds the adult looked only toward the object, for the next 10 seconds he varied between looking at the object and at the child, and in the last 10 seconds the adult talked about the problem and continued to look from the object to the child and back. There was no benefit to the child in helping: no reward was on offer in return for help. Furthermore, no appreciation was shown. What was the outcome? Ninety-two percent of the children helped at least once, whereas the figure was considerably lower in the control scenarios. In the scenario with the pen alone two-thirds of the children helped, compared to only a quarter in the control. Interestingly in almost all situations in which the toddler helped (84 percent), this happened in the first 10 seconds, without the adult looking at the toddler for help or asking for help. According to Warneken and Tomasello, their research shows that even very young children have a natural inclination to help others solve their problems, even when the other person is a stranger and there is nothing to be gained. They conclude that this is evidence of the existence of pure altruism.

Helpfulness is apparently in our genes, at least for most people. Not only are we able to tell when others need help at an early age, we are also prepared to help, even if the help offered in the experimental scenario did not take much effort and the children did not have to sacrifice much.

Daniel Batson and his team have carried out a great deal of research into the situations in which adults are altruistic. Their experiments show that people help others when they feel empathy for them, even when the costs are greater than the rewards. This empathy is generated when people see that the other needs help, when they value the well-being of the person in need, and when they are able to put themselves in the position of the other and to understand what the help means for them.

But do terms such as *altruism, empathy*, and *helping* have any implications for the workplace? Surely business is business? Certainly, but at the same time helping and serving often form the core of the work, the *raison d'être* of the organization. We see it, for example, in a company's mission statement, the formal statement of the company's ultimate higher goal. The pharmaceutical company GlaxoSmithKline, for instance, describes its mission as "to improve the quality of human life by enabling people to do more, feel better and live longer"; Microsoft's mission is "to help people realize their full potential"; and that of Phillips to "improve the quality of people's lives through the timely introduction of meaningful innovations." There's a good reason why the fundamental meaning of the term *economy* breaks down into "household (*eco-*) management (*-nomy*)." In this respect the chief executive of a bank hit the nail on the head when he described the function of banks as "serving the real economy."

This does not mean that working and doing business are purely altruistic, in the sense of "helping at any price and at all cost." If they were, businesses would soon go under. The art of working and doing business is creating win-win situations, in which people help one another while also helping themselves, and this should occur in the order of serving followed by earning. Serving may not necessarily lead *directly* to earning. Helpfulness resides precisely in those situations where a cost or sacrifice is involved. No ethics without pain. The fact that this pain leads to a warm glow is a bonus. In fact, it is something that should be cherished. It clearly comes from the heart and goes to the heart.

How do these great missions of helping and serving work out in practice? A bank director gave an example: "Our local banks are close to the community and the customer, so we have been customer-oriented for more than one hundred years. Once we throw in our lot with a customer, sometimes from father to son, then we support them for a long time. Even through the hard times. Then we try to reduce or postpone interest payments, for instance." That way you get customers for life.

5 What You Expect Is What You Get: The Pygmalion and Golem Effects

I once gave a workshop about integrity at work. The participants were members of the management team of a manufacturing company. Two of the managers were highly critical from the start: "It's all very well talking about norms and values, but the staff will fleece us given half a chance. Let me tell you what's gone on over the past year. If that's no proof of people's wickedness ... " A catalogue of reprehensible practices followed, such as theft, neglect, sabotage and intimidation. Two managers remained aloof. Cautiously, I asked them whether they recognized these practices within their own divisions. To everyone's surprise they said that they had experienced very few incidents. "Of course the shit occasionally hits the fan, but it's more the exception than the rule. As a rule I find my people pretty honest," said one of the two managers, rather proudly.

During the follow-up sessions elsewhere in the organization it became apparent that all of these managers were right. They got what they expected. The "Pygmalion effect" was at play: the way people are seen influences the way they are treated, consequently prompting them to act accordingly, and thus confirm the original view of them. In this way people set up a self-fulfilling prophecy, resulting in widely differing behavior within divisions of the same company.

The Pygmalion effect is named after the myth recounted by the Roman poet Ovid. He tells the story of Prince Pygmalion of Cyprus, who cannot find a woman he wants to marry. He therefore makes an ivory statue of his ideal woman. When he falls head over heals in love with this statue, he prays to Venus to bring it to life. Venus grants the prayer, and the prince and his wife live a long and happy life. Pygmalion's fantasy therefore becomes reality. This story inspired George Bernhard Shaw to write his 1913 play *Pygmalion*, the basis for the later musical *My Fair Lady*, in which Professor Higgins teaches an uneducated girl to speak and act like a true lady. What was seen as impossible was made possible by believing in it.

The Pygmalion effect was first researched by Robert Rosenthal and Lenore Jacobson. They carried out research at an American elementary school with 18 classes. At the start of the school year the children took an IQ test. The teachers received a list with the students who, in comparison to their classmates, were likely to make an intellectual leap in the coming eight months. The teachers assumed that the list was based on the results of the IQ test, but in reality it was a random selection of 20 percent of the students. There was actually no relation whatsoever between the students mentioned and the IQ test. The only difference between these children and the rest of the class was the assumption on the part of the teachers. After eight months the test was repeated with all the children.

In all classes tested it turned out that the IQ of the students labeled "promising" increased by at least 12 percent more than the other students. The children for whom expectations were high had made better progress in reality. It is worth noting that the teachers had not spent more time on these students. In fact, they had spent less time on them. So what explained the difference? The explanation was that the teachers, on the basis of their expectations, had subconsciously adjusted their behavior toward the students. Without realizing it, the teachers treated the students for whom they had higher expectations differently from the others. Rosenthal and Jacobson found four factors in which the selected students were treated differently. First, the teachers established a warmer social relationship with them, by giving them more personal and positive attention and support, and by talking to them in a different tone of voice, for example. Second, the teachers gave them more learning material at a higher level of difficulty, making them feel more challenged. Third, the teachers gave them more space in class to respond. And fourthly, the teachers provided them with more and higher quality feedback on their work, both verbally and nonverbally. As a result, the students behaved in accordance with the higher expectations of their teacher. This led to them achieving more.

Conversely the students of whom the teachers expected less felt less challenged and behaved accordingly. And because the teachers' expectations were not high, they were more easily satisfied with the students' achievements. In fact, the research revealed that the teachers felt put out when these students performed well. An unexpectedly good achievement therefore had a negative effect. The teachers did not reward this behavior, but punished it, because the students were not fulfilling their expectations. This is termed the Golem effect. Golem is a figure of Jewish legend. A robot-like being was created to eradicate evil, but eventually the golem itself becomes a monster; the more powerful it grows, the more evil it becomes.

All kinds of follow-up research has demonstrated these Pygmalion and Golem effects. What a manager thinks of employees is confirmed because the manager acts according to his expectations and employees react according to the behavior of the manager. This leads to a self-fulfilling prophecy.

The "problem" is that we create our own proof, thereby proving ourselves right. If people are regarded as criminals then they are treated as such, and the likelihood of them subsequently engaging in criminal behavior increases. The flipside is that positive expectations can lead to positive behavior. If people are seen as responsible, then they will also receive more responsibilities, leading them to behave more responsibly. It is therefore not so much a question of whether the chairman of the bank in Chapter 1 might *be* right, as that he will be *proven* right. Or put more conservatively, the chance of his employees behaving more honestly and responsibly will only increase if the chairman expresses his vision powerfully, consistently, and frequently. That happened in the manufacturing company described at the start of this chapter: the behavior of employees was the product of the expectations of their managers and not the other way round. This meant that the managers were continually confirmed in their belief, so that a negative, downward spiral was created in two divisions, and a positive, upward spiral in two others.

Expectations become reality, according to Rosenthal and Jacobson's research. There is a limit to what we can expect of expectations. We cannot use them as some kind of magic formula and thus control reality to the extent of turning every criminal into a philanthropist and vice versa. Reality is stubborn, but we must always be alert to the possibility of the Pygmalion and Golem effects.

The crucial point is to be aware of how our views of others influence their behavior. The view you have of people leads to those people behaving in a certain way, even if these expectations are never stated, and even when there are no expectations at all. Because a lack of expectations is an expectation in itself. And this kind of expectation is hardly likely to encourage someone to flourish.

6 Self-Image and Behavior: The Galatea Effect

In the previous chapter we saw how much our expectations of others determine their behavior. But it is not only other people's expectations which influence our behavior. The images and expectations we have *of ourselves* also have a role to play. This can have a powerful effect, even more powerful than the Pygmalion and Golem effects.

The images people form of themselves, and which determine their behavior, are termed the "Galatea effect," named after the ivory statue made by Pygmalion and brought to life by Venus. The effect refers to the fact that people who are convinced of their own abilities, for instance, are more successful. The more a salesperson believes in his own sales abilities and the quality of the product he is selling, the more successful he is in his sales. Here again the idea of the self-fulfilling prophecy applies. The belief becomes a reality. As Henry Ford, founder of the car manufacturer Ford, once said, "Whether you think you can, or you think you can't, you're right."

The same applies, up to a point, to the image people have of their own ethics. People who see themselves as bad, malicious, and untrustworthy will behave that way. And people who see themselves as honest, truthful, and trustworthy are more likely to behave well. Someone who sees himself as trustworthy, for example, will make more effort to fulfill this self-image, thus reinforcing his trustworthiness. And someone who sees himself as untrustworthy and attaches little value to promises and commitments will be more likely to let things slip and give up.

Kathleen Vohs and Jonathan Schooler researched how people's expectations of themselves determine their own behavior. They examined whether a change in self-image led to different behavior. They also researched whether people who saw themselves as "heteronomous" (a product of circumstances and lacking free will) or "autonomous" (immune to circumstances and possessing free will) were more susceptible to unethical behavior.

The researchers had the participants take a mathematics test on computers. They were told that due to a software error the answers might appear on the screen. To prevent this, the participants were asked to press the spacebar immediately for each new question. In reality the researchers observed whether the participants secretly used the answers, instead of doing the calculations themselves. Before the participants took the test, the researchers also did something else. They used an established method to imprint an idea on the participants (a process known as *priming* in the literature), in this case a conviction regarding free will. Some of the students were required to read an article stating that science refutes the notion of free will and that the illusion of free will is a product of the biochemical make-up of the brain. Other participants did not receive this reading material. In reading the article the first group was more inclined to believe that free will does not exist.

The results were clear. Those with a weaker conviction regarding free will (and therefore the extent to which they could determine their own behavior and future) were more inclined to cheat than those whose convictions were not influenced. The first group cheated approximately 45 percent more than the second group. If people see themselves as responsible, they will be more inclined to take responsibility and behave responsibly. If people can hide behind other factors, such as the idea that their will is preprogrammed and their behavior is predestined, they are more likely to behave dishonestly. In a second experiment it became apparent that the participants primed beforehand with the idea that people have free will were less inclined to steal money.

The research by Vohs and Schooler demonstrates not only that self-image determines behavior, but also the ease with which self-image, and subsequently behavior, can be influenced. Research shows that if we are primed to think of a library we talk more quietly, if we think of old age we walk more slowly, and if we think of professors we become cleverer. The activation of particular images automatically prompts associated behaviors. More on this in the following chapters.

So we not only shape ourselves according to the mold made for us by others, but also that which we make for ourselves. It is therefore important to examine one's self-image. Whether we see ourselves as playthings (heteronomous) or as players (autonomous) makes a difference to our behavior. If we see ourselves as heteronomous, we are more likely to succumb to pressure and temptation than if we see ourselves as autonomous. The same applies to organizations: employees who see themselves as a product of their environment bend with the wind and are unable to show any backbone. This then paves the way for unethical behavior, as a reaction to stiff competition, because the customer asks for it, or because the government issues incomprehensible laws. Ethical behavior likewise begins with a self-image of autonomy.

7 Self-Knowledge and Mirages: Self-Serving Biases and the Dodo Effect

A company with more than a thousand employees introduced a new assessment system, requiring all employees to assess themselves in advance of an appraisal, based on a five-point scale: (a) far below average, (b) below average, (c) average, (d) above average, and (e) far above average. After the whole assessment cycle was finished, one of the employees in human resources began to have misgivings. It was remarkable that there were hardly any complaints about the appraisal. She therefore decided to analyze the assessment figures. What did she discover? Eighty-seven percent of employees had judged themselves above or even far above average, and only 3 percent had placed themselves below or far below average. In itself this would not have been such a big problem, if the management had corrected the picture. But when the employee finally looked at the management's assessments, her surprise was even greater. Eighty-three percent of employees had received an appraisal result of above or far above average from their manager, and only 5 percent had a score far below or below average. This was strange, because average must be average, and statistically shouldn't there be as many people below as above average? Average was clearly not average. That aroused the employee's suspicions: was this a matter of fraud? Extensive inquiries among employees and managers showed her that they had acted in good faith. With a few exceptions everyone stood by their assessments. What explained this score?

A possible explanation lies in people's biases. People can have a distorted view of reality, because they cannot observe reality objectively. A large body of research shows that the majority of people see themselves as above average. The majority of people, for example, think themselves more intelligent, better looking, funnier, and better at driving than average. The majority also consider themselves more honest, more trustworthy, more ethical, more fair, more open, and more helpful than average. When married couples are asked about their own share of the household chores, the estimates often come out well above 100 percent. When scientists are asked about their own contribution to a jointly written article, again the sum often easily exceeds 100 percent. In the United States at least 90 percent of managers consider themselves to function above average. In that respect the company mentioned above was not so exceptional after all, but actually pretty "normal." This effect of overestimation is also called the "dodo effect," named after the passage in *Alice in Wonderland* in which the dodo, in response to the question who of all the animals won a running race, replies that "everyone won."

One reason that we are more positive about ourselves is that we are more intimately acquainted with ourselves and our achievements than with others and their achievements. A reason that we are more positive about people close to us than people we know less well, is that we know more about the achievements of those close to us. We have a better view of the achievements of colleagues in our own team than of colleagues in other teams. We not only see more and better, but we can also more easily remember our own achievements and those of the people close to us than those of others, because they make more of an impression on us and we store them better in our brains.

But even if we had a more neutral view of our achievements and those of others, we could still make an incorrect assessment. The way in which our brains process and filter information is susceptible to systematic errors. This occurs because our brains make use of heuristics, a kind of mental shortcut. We use this technique, for example, to interpret observations, to store and access them when we need them, to subsequently compare and make judgments and decisions on that basis. The advantage is that we can think and make decisions faster. The disadvantage is that it is not only the facts that come through, as the brain puts its own spin on observations, leading us to make errors in observations, memories, and attributing value.

Psychologists have long known that when people have a vested interest in something they have trouble seeing it without bias, even when they see themselves as honest. It is not uncommon for the trainers and supporters, for example, to think that theirs is the best team, regardless of the result of the match.

One of the biases observed is the self-serving bias. This bias protects our self-worth, self-confidence, and identity against negative influences. A positive self-image is important in order to survive; too much self-doubt is detrimental. The self-serving bias plays a role in the way in which we judge things. In "attribution theory" it is assumed that people are more likely to attribute success to their own talents and abilities (internal attribution), while they tend to attribute their failures to circumstances (external attribution). When a salesperson meets his sales targets, he will explain this as resulting from his intelligence, hard work or sales skills. And if the same salesperson does not achieve his goals, he will blame this on a bad market, insufficient support from the organization or bad luck. This removes the necessity of doubting his self-worth and self-image. Some people, generally unconsciously, make use of external attribution by framing the situation ahead of time in such a way that it can be used as an excuse later. This phenomenon is known as *self-handicapping*. An example is the salesperson intentionally spending too little time on his acquisition: if he still attains his sales target, he will attribute this to his special sales skills, because even with too little time he achieved the target. If he does not achieve the target, he will blame this on lack of time, to avoid having to doubt his sales skills.

Biases lead to what Ann Tenbrunsel and colleagues call "ethical mirages" and ultimately to a flattered self-image. We are less ethical than we think. This leads us to run various risks: because we overestimate ourselves and underestimate others, we are less open to criticism from others, less critical of ourselves, and we fail to properly understand ethical dilemmas and challenges. This also forms a breeding ground for feelings of injustice ("Why do I get the same as another, when I contributed much more?"). Because of these biases we take more, sometimes even unacceptable, risks ("The risks apply to others, not to me"), as in investing ("I'll beat the market, the other investors don't understand a thing"). This leads collaborations to go awry ("Why must all the initiative come from me? It's time someone else came up with an idea"). In this vein, research by Eugene Caruso and colleagues showed that the more participants see their individual contributions to a project coming to more than 100 percent in total, the less they are prepared to work together. The biases make us more egotistical in the eyes of others: if we think we have contributed more than is actually the case and we wish to reward ourselves accordingly, then the rest will see this as disproportionate. Moreover, others will see us as even more egotistical if they themselves have an inflated self-image and think that it was they who contributed more than the rest. For that reason we tend to be more suspicious of the motives of others than about our own motives and we consider others more self-centered than ourselves.

Biases are stubborn things. Once we have approached information in a distorted way, it is difficult to reinterpret the same information more evenhandedly. It is therefore important to be aware of the existence of biases. And especially the biggest bias of all: that we consider others more biased than ourselves.

It is possible to suppress biases. An example is so-called "unpacking," as shown by Eugene Caruso and colleagues. They asked MBA students to indicate which part of their group work they had done. The average total was 139 percent, but a simple intervention considerably reduced this bias. Before stating their own contribution, the participants were required to indicate the contribution of each of the other group members. After unpacking the total group work, the percentage fell to 121, almost halving the overestimate. Thinking of what another has done before looking at ourselves clearly makes a considerable difference.

8 Apples, Barrels, and Orchards: Dispositional, Situational, and Systemic Causes

"Away with that rotten apple, it'll spoil the whole barrel!" That was the reaction of the business sector when it became known that one company had showered officials on a large scale and over a long period with expensive presents, exotic trips, and payments in kind. This kind of reaction is normal. Where there is a suspicion of malpractice, the rotten apple must be tracked down and eliminated as quickly as possible. But is it really the case that a rotten apple will contaminate the rest?

Ray Fisman and Edward Miguel used data from what they describe as a "unique natural experiment" on the extent to which the culture of a country influences the corruption of inhabitants. Under "culture" we understand the collectively shared beliefs about right and wrong, what is permitted, and what is not. For this experiment they examined parking offences in New York by 1,700 UN diplomats from 146 different countries. And a good many offences there were too! Between November 1997 and November 2002 they had received more than 150,000 parking fines altogether. The reason for the high number is that until the end of 2002 diplomats and their families had immunity, a privilege which meant that their parking fines were waived. Because there were no sanctions on their behavior, Fisman and Miguel were able to examine whether the country of origin affected the number of fines that each diplomat had received in the five years. As a gauge for the culture of a country they used the corruption index of Transparency International, an organization which works to combat corruption worldwide. This index indicates a country's perceived corruption level. Countries such as New Zealand, Denmark, Sweden, and Singapore are seen as fairly clean, whereas countries such as Somalia, Afghanistan, and Burma are seen as corrupt. The researchers checked various points in advance, including the country's gross national product and the diplomat's salary, so that the relationship between the position of the country of origin in the corruption index and the number of parking fines could be calculated as accurately as possible.

Fisman and Miguel did indeed find a strong relationship. Diplomats from corrupt countries received considerably more parking fines than diplomats from non-corrupt countries. The diplomats from Kuwait took the prize. Over the five years they committed 249 parking offences per diplomat, followed by Egypt (141), Chad (126), and Sudan (121). The diplomats from countries such as Sweden and Denmark, however, received no parking fines at all. Apparently the culture of the country in which one is brought up affects one's morality, which in turn affects one's behavior, even if one resides in another country.

Experimental research by Abigail Barr and Danila Serra exhibits similar results. In all kinds of imaginary scenarios 285 participants from 43 countries were asked to state to what extent they would be prepared to slip an official some money in exchange for a tax reduction, preferential treatment in a legal case, or faster treatment in a hospital. Another part of the group had to decide, in the role of official, how likely they would be to accept the money in the different situations. Again it turned out that the nationality of the participant correlated with the extent to which bribes were offered and accepted. The higher the position of the country on Transparency International's corruption index, the higher the willingness to give and accept bribes.

Explaining people's behavior requires more than just the person's character, his "disposition": we must also understand the situation (for instance the fines for traffic offences) and the system (for instance the culture of the homeland). Corruption is not purely a question of rotten apples (contaminated or infected individuals). The barrel, or even the orchard, could be contaminated and spoil the apples. Corruption can be ingrained in the environment so that in the end everyone is infected with it. Just as humidity influences the extent of rot in the apples, the air quality in an organization (the organizational culture) influences the extent of corruption among employees, because employees are continually breathing this air in (and back out again). As the chairman of a research commission once concluded on corruption among the police, "It is sometimes less difficult for a new police officer to become corrupt than to remain honest."

It is important to examine what factors help and hinder the rotting process. We must also ask who is behind the barrels and the orchard. Who are the owners, growers, and pickers? Often these people remain out of range when scandals erupt. Furthermore it is important to establish who and what determine the quality of the apples. A fruit grower's task is not only to prevent rotting, but to cultivate apples of a high quality. In organizations it is therefore not so much a matter of preventing employees from becoming corrupt as ensuring that they flourish and bear fruit.

The more the environment is a determining factor, the more sensible it is to be reserved in condemning or praising individual people and organizations. In retrospect it became apparent that it was not just one company that was guilty of corruption. It was the rule rather than the exception in the sector as a whole. Furthermore, the competitor that first called for the rotten apple to be eliminated turned out to be the guiltiest of all. Corruption had become par for the course in that sector, and because it was seen as normal, people were blind to the risks that went with it. The eyes of those involved were only opened after the entire sector had owned up. As a director put it, "In court the scales fell from my eyes. It then became clear to me how blind we had all been all those years." Unfortunately, the damage had already been done.

Factor 1: Clarity

In the previous section we saw that not only character, but also environment, both situational and systemic, affects people's behavior. Since the organization for which someone works is also an environment, and therefore also influences their behavior, the question arises how far this influence stretches. As described in the introductory chapter, there are at least seven distinct factors within organizations which influence whether people do right or wrong.

The following eight chapters address the first factor: the clarity of norms, values, and responsibilities. Clarity relates to the extent to which the organization establishes clear expectations for directors, managers, and employees. The experiments reviewed show how environmental norms affect people's behavior.

In Chapter 9 we see how knowledge of norms influences behavior, while in Chapter 10 the issue of affinity with norms is discussed. We communicate norms in the way we name things, as will become clear in Chapter 11. Chapter 12 shows that norms can go over the top, whereas Chapter 13 shows that norms can in fact incite the opposite behavior. Besides being couched as formally written standards, norms are also present in behavior, as explained in Chapter 14, and in the design of the environment, as shown in Chapter 15. Chapter 16 explains how we can infer a person's norms and values from the state of their office, and subsequently how these affect the behavior of others.

9 Flyers and Norms: Cognitive Stimuli

In Chapter 8 it was shown that culture influences people's behavior. However, even if the norms of responsible and irresponsible behavior are clearly evident, people are not necessarily aware of them and do not necessarily behave accordingly. Norms can be present at the back of our minds but still be forgotten at the crucial moment. It is therefore important that this latent sense of values is activated. Research by Robert Cialdini and colleagues explains how this works and its implications.

Cialdini and colleagues observed visitors to a local library in the American state of Arizona. After each visitor stepped out of the car and entered the library, they placed a flyer under the windscreen wiper on the driver's side. The researchers then hid and waited until the visitor returned to the car. What would he do with the flyer after reading it? Would he throw it into the street, in violation of an evident norm, or would he behave well and take it with him in the car? There was no trash can in sight.

The researchers had flyers with five different texts. The flyer with the text "April Is Arizona's Fine Art's Month. Please Visit Your Local Art Museum" was thrown on the ground by 25 percent of the visitors. This flyer created a control situation, because the text on it had nothing to do with throwing the flyer away. The flyer with the text "April Is Arizona's Voter Awareness Month. Please Remember That Your Vote Counts" was thrown away less often. This text indirectly triggered the subjects' environmental awareness, as evidenced by the fact that only 22 percent of the flyers were thrown into the street. The flyer with the text "April Is Conserve Arizona's Energy Month. Please Turn Off Unnecessary Lights" was more concretely related to awareness of the environment, and led to only 17.5 percent of the visitors throwing their flyer on the ground. The flyer with the text "April Is Preserve Arizona's Natural Resources Month. Please Recycle" was thrown into the street even less, at 15 percent. Flyers with the text "April Is Keep Arizona Beautiful Month. Please Do Not Litter" were thrown away the least at only 10 percent.

This simple experiment shows that the flyer with the nonnormative message, which therefore had no association with good or bad, was the least effective in influencing normative behavior. It also shows that the more concrete the norm, the bigger the effect. This is another example of priming (see Chapter 6), or "cognitive activation": our brains are stimulated by reading the text, activating ideas, and concepts. Because the semantically overlapping concepts are related by neural networks in the human brain, the activation of one concept leads to activation of others. For example when a person thinks of a dog, related concepts such as "puppies," "wolves," and "cats" are activated in the brain. By drawing attention to a value in the experiment, there was a greater chance that the values semantically related to it would be activated in the brain. The greater the semantic proximity, the more effective the activation.

According to Cialdini and his team, their research also demonstrates that norms are only effective when they come together in the decisive moment (in this case the moment that the visitor decided whether or not to throw away the flyer). It is therefore important for organizations not only to establish values and communicate them, but also to ensure that these are activated at the right moment to nudge employees in the right direction. Training courses, for example, are often a bombardment of stimuli, but if the new knowledge is not regularly activated at the right moment, it is insufficiently used and fades.

It is currently fashionable to manage organizations on the basis of values and principles. Broad, abstract principles are often used, such as "customer focus," "integrity," "professionalism," "entrepreneurship," and "sustainability." However, it is questionable whether managers and employees can interpret what these mean for their behavior in a given situation. It takes a good number of steps to translate the core value of "sustainability" into concrete actions such as "separation of waste," "awareness of energy usage," and "recycling." We cannot take it for granted that people understand the meaning of the principle of "doing honest business" as it applies to pricing, exchange of information, and making agreements with competitors. Cialdini and colleagues' research shows that people get lost. Managing on the basis of values and principles therefore must not be allowed to mean that employees are left to their own devices.

10 The Ten Commandments and Fraud: Affective Stimuli

In the previous chapter we saw the importance of cognitive stimulation, where the chance that people follow a given norm increases the more concrete the communicated norm is. But this kind of activation can also deliver the desired behavior by a different path. Research by Nina Mazar and colleagues illustrates this point.

The participants of their experiment were asked to complete as many exercises as possible in 4 minutes. Each question consisted of a list of 12 numbers under 10, all with 2 decimal places. The participants were required to find 2 numbers which, added together, came to 10 exactly. Only one combination was possible. Participants were informed that a number of them, selected at random, would receive 10 dollars for every correct answer. This is a common set-up, but the researchers made their own addition: before the experiment half of the participants were required to write down 10 books they had read. The other half had to write down the Ten Commandments (insofar as they knew them). Half the group were informed in advance that they would be required to hand in their tasks afterwards to be examined by the researchers. The other half of the group were required to check their tasks themselves.

For the answers examined, the number of correctly completed questions was three on average. There was no difference between the group that wrote down books they had read and the group that listed the Ten Commandments. This evidently had no effect on performance. But what happened to the participants who were required to state themselves how many questions they had completed correctly? They were not checked and therefore had every opportunity to cheat. The participants who had written a list of books on average claimed to have completed just over four questions, at least a third more, which was clearly cheating. How many did the participants who had been asked to list the Ten Commandments claim? On average they reported having completed three tasks, as many as the participants with no opportunity to cheat.

Writing the Ten Commandments primed the participants' awareness of their own sense of honesty. This stimulus was so strong that all dishonesty disappeared. A nudge in the direction of honesty is apparently sufficient to get people to be honest, at least in the experimental scenario. It did not even matter how many commandments the participants could remember and write down, nor whether or not they were believers. Just thinking about them made a difference.

A little reminder can therefore make the difference between honesty and dishonesty. Like the experiment in the previous chapter, this suggests that it is not just a matter of knowing what is right and wrong, but also of thinking of the meaning and significance of honesty in the moment of temptation. In this experiment it was not so much a matter of cognitive priming, but more of "affective priming." The affect is activated. Thinking of the Ten Commandments gets people to stop and think about the importance of values, stimulating the will and motivation to keep to them. It activates the self-image of an honest, trustworthy person. Cheating at tasks is at odds with this image.

It is therefore important for organizations to affectively prime people. This works pretty well in general: all kinds of signs, symbols, and rituals emphasize the prevailing standards. Giving one's initials or a signature, for example, creates a moment in which the concept of responsibility is activated, as does working through a checklist or step-by-step plan. The trick is to make the nudge at the right moment, and in the right way. Whenever people sign a paper unthinkingly or check off an item on autopilot, that's an indication that the stimulus no longer works. When too much nudging goes on, the desired affect can turn to irritation. But many organizations do less than the optimum, allowing opportunities to slip by. In many professional groups and organizations, for example, an oath or promise is made once only, when this could happen periodically. A code of conduct could be brought to people's attention at every meeting, rather than once a year (e.g., by splitting it up into different sections). In that respect many churches do better than other organizations in reading out the Ten Commandments every Sunday.

In an experiment similar to Mazar's, the result was even more significant: the participating students were required to sign a form in which they declared that they would follow the code of conduct of the university throughout the experiment. In this case, again, there was considerably less cheating than when participants were not required to sign. What was remarkable was that the university did not even have a code. The implication that there was a code was clearly sufficient in itself. The implication of this study for us is not, however, that all codes of conduct could be dispensed with and that it is sufficient to *say* that one exists. This would in itself not be ethical.

11 The Name of the Game: Euphemisms and Spoilsports

At the end of 2010 it emerged that a man named Daniel had been degraded and tortured by colleagues in a factory over a period of 10 years. Daniel was tied down on a pallet while a colleague pushed his genitals into his face. They locked him in a cage, poured 25 kilos of talcum powder over him, and went to work on him with a pressure washer. His colleagues found this completely unremarkable. One of them, Lucien, claimed it was "normal in the company." It happened frequently. That's why Lucien was filming when Daniel was mistreated. He thought of it as "joking around" rather than bullying.

What happened here is a common occurrence: the use of euphemisms strips unethical practices of their moral connotations. Bribery becomes "oiling the wheels" or "service costs," stealing becomes "pinching" and "freeloading" and sleeping at work (something 42 percent of Americans admit to having done) becomes "recharging" or "having a quiet moment." By labeling things differently we take the ethical sting out of them and make them acceptable, normal, or even desirable. Bullying is wrong, but if it is defined as "joking around" then it becomes a social activity. So, for the sake of being sociable, Daniel's colleagues tied him to a pallet, laughed about it, and filmed him so they could enjoy it again later. According to Albert Bandura, who has written on this topic, euphemisms are a dangerous weapon. They close people's eyes and ears to what is morally questionable.

It is therefore important to remain alert to the use of euphemisms and to be quick to address them. Fraudulent practices can be allowed to hide behind terms such as "earnings management," "creative bookkeeping," and "financial engineering." Terms such as "trimming," "adjusting," "reshaping," and "slimming down" can be used to rationalize a wave of redundancies. And terms such as "slip-up," "side effects," and "externalities" can cover serious incidents, abuses, and reprehensible damage. Projects and programs can also have apparently innocent or even humorous names, while it is clear to insiders that shady dealings are involved. The energy company Enron, for example, used all kinds of names for strategies to manipulate the energy market in California. "Death Star" referred to transfer of energy in the opposite direction to demand, causing congestion on the grid. Enron then received money from the state for rectifying the congestion, which it achieved by transferring the energy in the right direction. "Fat Boy" stood for the transfer of more energy than the customers needed and subsequent delivery of the remainder to state businesses with a shortage at a higher price. A "Ricochet" referred to a process of purchasing energy in California, subsequently selling it to an intermediary outside the state, importing it back at a somewhat higher price, and finally selling it for a very high price in California, because there was a large energy deficit. At this time the forests of California were on fire and traders were celebrating because this drove up the price of energy. A trader spoke the legendary words: "Burn, baby, burn. That's a beautiful thing."

On the one hand we can use language to free bad behavior of its moral connotations, and on the other hand we can invent terms precisely to get a moral message across. Varda Liberman and colleagues carried out an experiment that demonstrates that a name can influence our behavior. The participants were invited to play a game. Half were told that they were going to play the "Wall Street Game" and the other half were told they would be playing the "Community Game." Both games were exactly the same. The only difference was the name. The researchers investigated the extent to which the players were competitive (tried to trump other players) or cooperative (tried to help other players).

Of the participants playing the Wall Street Game, almost two-thirds played competitively. In the Community Game the figure was just one-third, 50 percent less. The researchers had assessed the participants in advance as to their tendency to compete or cooperate. The competitive participants turned out not to be more competitive than the cooperative participants in either game. In fact, the competitive participants were even a little more cooperative in the Community Game.

Names send a powerful message as to what behavior is accepted, and therefore influence behavior. As in the previous chapters, it turns out that small changes can have significant consequences. Just giving the game a different name determines whether two-thirds of the players are competitive or cooperative. The names we give things state not only how we see them, but also how we and others *should see* them, which subsequently influences behavior. Do we speak, for example, of our "manager," "boss," "superior," "leader," or "president"? Do we talk about a "customer," "client," "buyer," or "consumer"? When, for example, in the education system a student is referred to as the "consumer" or "customer," this has a powerful effect: describing students in this way encourages them and their teachers to behave accordingly. Students will then see themselves as king ("The customer is king") and teachers will do anything to please students, for example, entertaining them during lectures and setting easy exams.

Speaking of games, it is dangerous to see work, business, and management as games. Thomas Watson, the founder of IBM, once said, "Doing business is a game, the greatest game in the world if you know how to play it." At the time of the financial crisis, a financial institution wrote that investment was a game. Seeing it this way created the impression it was a case of people amusing themselves, with made-up rules and nothing to lose, when in actual fact these are serious matters, with significant human interests on the line. People who see their work as a game would be better off at home playing Monopoly. Organizations need spoilsports, people who expose euphemisms for what they are.

12 Hypegiaphobia: The Fear Factor of Rules

"We are 40 percent *overcompliant*; we have 40 percent too many rules. The whole organization is riddled with them." These were the words of the director of a large organization on the eve of a process of change which liberally slashed the rules. Isn't this risky? Rules prevent incidents, don't they? If an incident arises despite them, then at least one can appeal to the offender on the basis of the rule? Or is there an optimum number of rules after which, as the director put it, an organization becomes riddled with them?

Research by Tal Katz-Navon and colleagues shows that the director's thinking is not so crazy after all. In their research they scrutinized the level of detail of the rules in 47 departments in different Israeli hospitals. They collected data for each department regarding the number of incidents occurring in operations and other treatment procedures over a year. The focus was on mistakes such as medication errors or mixing up test results. The incidents could cause the patient considerable injury and even be life-threatening.

What did the researchers find? In departments with few rules there were 13 incidents on average. The more departmental rules, the fewer incidents there were, down to an average of 9. This was the good news. Rules are useful. But what did the researchers find when they delved deeper? As the number of rules increased further, the number of incidents also increased, to an average of 21. The relationship between rules and incidents was not linear but curvilinear (a U-curve).

On the one hand, rules are useful; they ensure clarity and consistency. They allow people to get a grip on what they should be doing. On the other hand, rules can also pass a tipping point and be counterproductive. How does this come about? One possible explanation is what is known as "hypegiaphobia" (pronounced high-ped-jia-fobia), which means fear of taking responsibility. In the first instance rules lead to certainty, but too many rules have the opposite effect. People become afraid of breaking them. The more rules, the greater the chance that one will be forgotten, and the greater the chance of doing something wrong. People become obsessed; the rules become a goal in themselves. As long as the rules are adhered to, all is well. The patient may be dead, but at least the operation went according to plan. People become hesitant, stop thinking critically, and hide behind the rules. As a board member of a bank said, "If there's a problem, the solution may appear to be more rules, but I don't believe that's true. If you tell people exactly what they can do, they stop thinking. Then they take the attitude: 'I'll soon hear about it if I do something wrong.'" Too many rules are an impediment to taking responsibility. The more rules, the greater the moral license, because if it's not defined in the many rules, then it must be allowed.

The problem with hypegiaphobia is often even bigger in organizations in which the managers think they can prevent incidents, mistakes, and irregularities with even more rules. This further increases fear among employees, leading to an increase, not a decrease, in incidents. The increase in incidents proves to the management that the employees cannot be trusted, making the managers themselves more anxious. Many organizations fall prey to a tsunami of rules, leading to swelling contracts, codes of conduct stretching to 80 pages, often containing all kinds of specific regulations, and piles of procedures. A large pharmaceutical company recently counted the number of pages of internal regulations and codes which applied to employees. It came to 900 pages. Another example is a bank which recently came up with a dress code. Once they had started to set down on paper how employees should dress, there was no stopping them. If one thing is not permitted, then really neither is another. Otherwise, so they thought, employees would assume items not mentioned in the rules were permitted. A fast-growing code was created, culminating in 40 pages of detailed rules: employees were only permitted to wear skin-colored underwear, which did not show through their outer clothing and was not visible on the surface; employees who dyed their hair must ensure that their natural roots were not visible; men must have their hair trimmed monthly; black nail varnish was prohibited; there must be no garlic or onion odor on the breath, to give just a few examples.

For organizations the task is to find the balance between rules and personal responsibility for employees. What is optimal? It is not just a matter of preventing incidents, but also of achieving innovation, customer focus, and efficiency. Here too, a U-curve, this time inverted, applies. And here too the questions is whether an organization is in balance, and if not, whether the organization is left (too few rules) or right (too many rules) of the optimum.

So it was not so silly of the organization mentioned in the first paragraph of this chapter to cut back heavily on its rules. How can the optimum be achieved? Not, as is sometimes attempted, by gradually paring away at the list, for instance by getting rid of a rule at each meeting. This organization did it differently: the management first discovered the source of the multiplicity of rules, namely mistrust of employees and external stakeholders. Working now from the perspective of trust, rather than mistrust, they were able to determine which rules were really necessary. The rest of the rules were eliminated in one go, resulting in an increased sense of responsibility throughout the organization. Pruning the rules can allow employees to grow and flourish.

13 Rules Create Offenders and Forbidden Fruits Taste the Best: Reactance Theory

"If you beep you can't come in. Rules are rules." The prison director's words were final, so female lawyers visiting the prison went without their bras. What was going on? All visitors had to pass a metal detector at the prison entrance. If the device beeped, the visitors were required to get rid of the offending material, such as belts and loose change, and walk through the gate again. The detectors were so sensitively tuned that they also began to beep for very small metal objects, such as the metal underwires in bras. The management insisted that the metal detector worked perfectly and that rules were rules. The warders therefore demanded that the female lawyers take off their bras before entering the prison.

Just as we saw in the previous chapter, fear and uncertainty among the prison management led to "beeping" at everything, and they lost sight of common sense. It clearly shows a lack of respect to demand that female lawyers take off their bras and walk around the prison without them.

On the one hand this event is exceptional (although at a nearby prison experiencing similar exaggerated beeping, the story was that the warders themselves set off the device for young, attractive lawyers). On the other hand, all kinds of workplace rules can be experienced as stifling and intimidating. There are organizations where employees are not permitted to receive any business gift whatsoever, not so much as a ballpoint pen, where all nonwork-related websites are inaccessible, and where people can be sacked for making a phone call in the car, even if it is for work purposes. In such cases, organizations not only run the risk of employees becoming anxious and suffering from hypegiaphobia, there is another risk which brings these rules hurtling back like a boomerang.

James Pennebaker and Deborah Sanders wanted to know what effect prohibitions had on people's behavior. What happens, for example, if a sign is put up stating that graffiti on the wall is prohibited? How effective is this, and what factors does its effectiveness depend on? They placed two kinds of signs at eye level in the public toilets of a university. One contained a threatening text: "Do NOT Write on the Walls!" The other took a milder tone: "Please, do not write on the walls." What did the researchers discover when they went to register how much graffiti had been sprayed on the walls? Around the first sign, which was more threatening, there was much more graffiti than at the second sign.

A similar experiment was carried out by Joseph Grandpre. When students of a middle and secondary school were told not to smoke, the chance increased that they would do so, and when they were told that they must smoke, they smoked less.

Both studies show that the clearer and more threatening an order or prohibition, the greater the chance that the opposite will be done. *Rules create offenders.* But can we explain this? Jack Brehm developed "reactance theory" for this purpose. This theory suggests that people resent threats to their freedom. The sense of restricted freedom arouses resistance. The more people believe they are able to decide for themselves what is right, the stronger this feeling becomes. People try to reduce the unpleasant feeling (reactance) by exhibiting the opposite behavior and thereby winning back their freedom. For instance, people will start smoking if it is prohibited, to restore their threatened freedom of choice. Forbidden fruits taste the best because they taste of freedom.

Reactance theory applies just as much to adults as to teenagers. If people are not permitted to receive business gifts at work, then they have gifts delivered to them at home, and then they won't stop at the ballpoint pen. If private sites are shut off, then people will do anything to circumvent security and visit them more than if they were open to the public. People may also work off their rebellious feelings by working to rule. If people are not permitted to surf for personal use during work time, then they will stop doing anything for work outside work time. Stifling rules can also lead to overt rebellion or civil disobedience. In the prison situation, for example, some lawyers intentionally wore lots of metal objects, to frustrate the system. People find creative ways of easing their reactance. If spray painting is not permitted, then they go to work with felt-tips or brushes. If they are not allowed to write, then they take to glue or nails. If not this wall, then another, where there's no sign. This effect is also exhibited among motorcyclists: after riding on routes with permanent speed checks, where they consider the maximum speed unreasonably low, they ride extra fast in the areas where there are no checks, to recover their sense of freedom. The rules really only transfer the problem. This is the so-called "waterbed effect": where you press (where attention is focused), the water (the problem) goes down, only to push up elsewhere.

It is therefore important to examine the effect of rules on oneself and others, to watch out for restrictive and pedantic rules, and those which now seem pointless. In a comedy sketch, John Cleese plays a character wishing to enter a casino. The doorman refuses because he is not wearing a tie. Rules are rules. Shortly afterwards he returns, and again the doorman refuses him entrance, this time because the tie is too short. Rules are rules. Shortly afterwards Cleese again appears at the entrance, now with a long tie, and no other clothing. And because there are no further rules, the doorman now lets him in. As far as I know, the lawyers from the example at the beginning of the chapter did not have to resort to this to open the eyes of the management; the commotion in the media put a stop to the peepshow.

14 What Happens Normally Is the Norm: Descriptive and Injunctive Norms

Expectations of desirable behavior can be put down in writing. For instance most large businesses and government agencies have a code of conduct stating how managers and employees should behave. However, in practice other factors, such as the physical environment, determine the norm. Robert Cialdini and his colleagues also researched this issue.

Once again their experiment involved flyers. This time the subjects were visitors to a hospital. On returning from a visit the subject found a flyer under the windscreen on the driver's side of the car. It was so large that visitors could not really drive away with it in place. On the flyer was the text: "This is automotive safety week. Please drive carefully." There was no trash can nearby. Unnoticed, the researchers registered what the visitor did with the flyer. This time it was not the flyer text which the researchers varied, but the environment: for half the visitors the parking lot floor was covered with flyers, sweet wrappers, cigarette butts, and paper cups; for the other half the floor was clean.

In the clean environment, 14 percent of the visitors threw their flyer on the ground, and in the messy environment the figure more than doubled, to 32 percent. This was not all the researchers did. What would happen in the parking lot if a passer-by dropped a flyer in full sight, a few meters from the visitor? In a littered environment the figure for flyers thrown on the ground rose from 32 to 54 percent. Compared with the clean environment in which the passer-by did not throw anything on the ground, almost four times as many people threw the flyer away!

This experiment shows nicely how people read norms from their environment, both directly, according to what they see others doing (whether a passer-by throws a flyer on the floor), and indirectly, through the consequences of what others have done (whether the environment is dirty or clean). According to Cialdini and colleagues, there are both "injunctive" norms, norms which prescribe the desired behavior, and "descriptive" norms, norms which describe the current behavior. People are influenced not only by how things *should be*, but also how they *are*.

From an early age people imitate others. Our talent for this is down to our mirror neurons. A few days after birth, babies will already stick out their tongues when others do so, and cry when they hear another baby crying. Later on we laugh when others laugh, and suffer pain when others suffer pain (at least when the others are people we love). When we look at what someone else is doing, we carry out the action in our thoughts. We copy behavior because this offers us something to hold onto in a world of uncertainty and unknowns. It makes life easier, because we don't always have to think for ourselves. We also have a "normative need": other people are more willing to accept us if we endorse their actions and go along with them than if we reject them and distance ourselves. As a politician said about mores within politics, "If you don't know how it should be done, then you don't belong here." That's why we observe what others do.

If other people do something in a particular way, then we quickly interpret this as a sensible thing to do. In a dirty environment the descriptive norm is that it is acceptable to throw litter into the street, and that this is also perfectly sensible, because it will be cleaned up (so we tell ourselves, even if the state of the environment suggests otherwise), or you have more important things to do (such as hurrying to get somewhere on time), or people will give you funny looks if you go in search of a trash can. This descriptive norm does not alter the fact that there is an injunctive norm which tells people not to throw litter into the street. When the injunctive and descriptive norms conflict, the question is which takes priority. The more the descriptive norm imposes itself, the greater the chance that this is followed. The more you are surrounded by speeding cars, the greater the chance that you too will exceed the speed limit. In the case of the experiment, the greater the mess in the parking lot, the greater the chance that your own flyer too will end up on the ground. It's easy to come up with an excuse: everyone does it, so I do too.

The message is that it is worth ensuring a "clean" environment, both literally and figuratively: physical clutter within the organization will only cause more clutter, and an organization which makes a mess of things, will encourage behavior among employees and outsiders which will lead to more mess. If you set a good example, others will follow. That's why a clean environment is important.

And note the following: if it has to be messy, make sure it's at least a well-organized mess. In the experiment, when the dirt was swept up into three big piles, only 18 percent of visitors threw their flyer on the floor. If you have lots of papers in your room, then at least put them in neat piles. If there are many incidents in your organization, keep track of them by categorizing them.

Second, if there is still a mess, do not immediately announce that mess is prohibited. Experiments by Kees Keizer show that whenever a prohibition sign is placed in a littered environment, more people throw trash into the street. Almost a third more violated the regulation. Prohibition signs work against themselves if the environment sends out a different message, because it focuses people's attention more on the traces of behavior in violation of the norms. The divide between the injunctive and descriptive norm will only become larger, and the injunctive norm will come off worse. The task is therefore to tidy up the mess, before communicating that others should refrain from making a mess.

15 Broken Panes Bring Bad Luck: The Broken Window Theory

In the 1980s and 1990s the New York City police were confronted with increasing rates of theft, violent crime, and drug sales in the city. In order to combat this, the police launched the "Quality of life" campaign. The idea behind this was that a littered environment was a feeding ground for criminality. An environment with social disorder (such as loitering youths, public drunkenness, and prostitution) and physical disorder (such as graffiti, abandoned buildings, and trash in the street) increased the chance of both petty and serious crime. For this reason graffiti and traces of vandalism were removed and, mindful of the message of the previous chapter, the litter in the streets was cleaned up. To the delight of the police, crime figures in the city dropped significantly.

The explanation was termed the "broken window theory." James Wilson and George Kwelling propose that when a window in a building is broken and goes unrepaired, the chance of another window breaking increases. The more broken windows, the greater the chance of more windows being smashed to smithereens. A building with broken windows subsequently attracts other forms of criminality, such as breaking in, squatting, and stripping the building. This in turn will cause criminality around the building to increase; it attracts criminals, while law-abiding citizens avoid the area. According to the broken window theory, people see physical and social disorder as a sign that everything is permissible and that authority is absent. Such an environment puts ideas into people's heads, and lowers the threshold to overstepping their boundaries. The underlying idea is that a single transgression encourages people to commit further transgressions or expands to become one big transgression, and that one transgressor grows into many.

Empirical evidence for this theory was supplied years later by Kees Keizer and colleagues. In one experiment the main entrance to a parking lot was temporarily closed by the researchers. However, they had left a gap of 50 centimeters. On the fence the researchers had hung up a sign with the text "No entry, go around to the other entrance." The side entrance was 200 meters further on. What would people do when they wanted to get to their cars, walk around, or slip through the opening? The researchers were curious in particular as to whether the behavior of the drivers would depend on the environment. For that reason they had hung up another board on the fence with the text, "No locking bicycles to the fence." In one scenario there were four bicycles 1 meter from the fence. In the other there were four bicycles locked directly to the fence. In the environment with the freestanding bicycles, 27 percent of the people slipped through the fence; with the bicycles locked to the fence the figure was 82 percent. The researchers had expected this effect, but were surprised by the big difference.

In another experiment, Keizer and colleagues examined whether the negative effect of such an environment could spur people on to more serious misdemeanors. This time the researchers stuffed an addressed envelope half way into a red letterbox. A five-euro bill was clearly visible through the window of the envelope. Would passers-by take the letter out and pocket the money? In a clean environment 13 percent did this. When there was graffiti around the letterbox, the figure doubled to 27 percent.

The explanation which Keizer and colleagues gave was the following. They distinguished three goals for influencing behavior: "normative goals" (behaving as you should), "hedonic goals" (feeling good), and "gain goals" (improving your material situation). These three goals do not always weigh equally; their relative weight is affected by the environment. The normative goal, however, is a priori the weakest of the three and is under pressure from the two other goals. Environmental factors, such as disorder, push normative goals to the background, bringing the other goals to the fore. If someone sees that others give the normative goal less priority, that reduces their own attention for the goal, and laziness and greed gain the upper hand. If you notice that others violate the rules (for instance by locking their bicycles to the fence when this is explicitly prohibited), then yourself will attach less importance to the normative goal of behaving properly, increasing the chance that you will slip through the fence. If you see an envelope containing five euros hanging out of a letterbox, then the disordered environment increases the weight you give to your own gain goal, so you are more likely to take the envelope. Violation of norms spreads because the normative goal (following the rules) is weakened, opening up more space for self-interest.

The strength of this theory is that it shows that people not only imitate the behavior of others (as shown in the previous chapter in Cialdini's research), but that when people observe others violating the norms, this also leads them to violate other norms. The normative goal is weakened in its entirety. This means that in order to prevent an escalation of violations, minor misdemeanors and their visible effects should be dealt with quickly, and that if you want to improve the ethics and integrity of an organization, this must be done in an integrated and coherent way. If an organization wishes to combat internal fraud, then it must also prevent antisocial behavior such as intimidation, aggression, and hostility. If an organization wishes to deal carefully and responsibly with clients, then it must deal carefully with other stakeholders. Unethical behavior is very difficult to isolate: an organization cannot be ethical in one relationship or situation, and unethical in another. Unethical behavior, as shown in the above experiments, is a wildfire that spreads easily.

Keizer's theory also helps to explain why, if unethical behavior has escalated and spread widely, this cannot be reversed simply by cleaning up afterwards. The culture is then already so badly infected that people no longer attach any significance to the normative goal. Much energy must then be put into establishing and communicating the importance of this. Companies which have slipped off the rails and been discredited can therefore make a good start towards recovery by re-evaluating their business mission from a normative perspective, reformulating business goals, rewriting the code of conduct, making intensive efforts to communicate this, and providing extensive training to employees. This is the only way to win back territory for the normative goal, and it will improve behavior on countless fronts in its wake.

If you want to prevent an organization being derailed and a great deal of energy being required to get things back on track, then the task is to repair "broken windows" in the organization as quickly as possible.

16 The Office as a Reflection of the Inner Self: Interior Decoration and Architecture

The director of a regulatory body works with a pistol on the table. Literally. She keeps a pistol on the meeting table in her office, a model that looks like it came straight out of a western. Fortunately it is made of porcelain and encased in plastic. For her the pistol is innocent: "I had the opportunity to choose a work of art, and I thought this was really beautiful." But do her visitors feel the same way?

Leonard Berkowitz and Anthony Lepe researched whether the presence of a weapon in a room influences behavior. The participants were subjected to the irritation of being made to wait a long time before the experiment began, and they were subsequently required to administer a shock to another participant. Half of the participants waited in a room in which a weapon had been placed, as if carelessly left behind, in a corner. For the other half a badminton racket stood in its place. The researchers registered the duration of shocks administered by the subjects. What did they discover? In the cases where the badminton racket had been present, the shock on average lasted a third of a second. When there was a weapon present, the shock lasted 50 percent longer on average. According to the researchers, objects in the environment can arouse particular behavior, just as an innocent unloaded weapon in their experiment led to more aggression. These objects work as stimuli: they stimulate the brain and evoke particular associations and behavior.

The accessories in someone's office can therefore influence the behavior of visitors. A pistol in the office, even a fake, could lead to more aggressive behavior on the part of visitors. Likewise the director with a punch ball hanging in his room will have to take into account more aggression from his visitors. And the director with a fruit machine in his room should not be too surprised if visitors take more risks.

On the other hand, the set-up of one's office says something about the inner self: about who we are, what we consider important, and how we are put together. Samuel Goslinga and colleagues have shown that conclusions regarding a person's character can be drawn from personal spaces, at home, and at work. The participants in their research were able to draw conclusions about a stranger's character based on their office or bedroom.

Research by Andrew Lohman and colleagues shows that the interior decoration of couples' living rooms speaks volumes about the quality of their relationship. In their research the participants were required to sit in the room where they would normally welcome guests at home. They were then required to point out their favorite objects in the room, and asked which objects they most wanted guests to notice. Finally the couples noted which objects were acquired individually and which together. The research showed that the better the bond between the couples, the more they wanted guests to notice objects which they had acquired together. Furthermore the better the relationship the more the favorite objects had been acquired together. So if you are interested in the strength of your relationship, you could sit down on your couch at home and examine the extent to which you both want the same objects to be seen by guests and whether you acquired these objects together.

What applies in private also applies at work. The manager who plasters an image of the sales figures of the past five years over the entire wall of his office shows that he values sales. The employee who displays all kinds of prizes clearly sees success and scores as important. Anyone with multiple family photos probably has good family relationships. A cluttered workplace or office suggests that the person who works there is cluttered too. A tidy workspace, on the other hand, says that the person is a perfectionist and has his work under control.

Inspecting the offices of an organization can yield a great deal of information about its culture. The CEO's office alone says a great deal about values and norms. What are the dimensions, colors, layout, objects? Is the room on the top floor or on the ground floor? Is it decorated with personal items? In carrying out such an inspection you must, of course, be prepared to dig below the surface; a tidy room says nothing if there is chaos behind closed cabinet doors. If this is the case across much of the rest of the organization, then that is a red flag, because it increases the likelihood that people think this way about the products they sell and the figures they publish. The next time you walk into your office, it might be interesting to look around with a visitor's eye and ask yourself what the room says about you and your relationship with the organization.

The same goes for the architecture and general state of repair of office buildings. In buildings where the paint is peeling, outward appearance apparently is not the highest priority. Buildings which rise high above the surrounding properties imply pride. Buildings with lots of glass clearly suggest that the banner of transparency flies high, unless it is reflective glass, in which case there is nothing to be seen of what goes on inside. Many organizations recently toppled by malpractice had head offices with only reflective glass. Coincidence?

Factor 2: Role-Modeling

In the previous section we saw that it is important for an organization both to establish the desired norms, values, and responsibilities and to effectively communicate these so that directors, managers, and employees know what is expected. This communication not only occurs in writing, but also in action and in the set-up of the work environment.

People read the norms applicable to them from the behavior of others, especially their role models. Within organizations these are line managers, higher management, and directors. Role-modeling is therefore the second factor which affects behavior in organizations. This was touched on in Chapter 14.

The following six chapters discuss experiments which illustrate the meaning of role-modeling. Chapter 17 shows what ethical leadership involves and how powerful role-modeling can be. It is not only down to the behavior employees see in their leaders, but also to what the management task them to do. Chapter 18 examines obedience and the risks attached to it. Having shown that role-modeling depends on how the management see themselves, Chapter 19 then examines the effect of this on those being managed. On the one hand managers should give a good example; on the other hand they are in a position in which they are more likely to abuse their authority. In Chapters 20 and 21 we see where this can lead. The final chapter of this section shows that model behavior can also lead to the opposite behavior in others.

17 The Need for Ethical Leadership: Moral Compass and Courage

Like radars, people search their surroundings for signals which indicate how they should behave. Research shows that seeing someone in the street give something to a collector increases the chance that we too will give, and if someone throws rubbish into the street, the chance increases that we will do the same. Both good and bad examples apparently have followers. Will we follow just anyone's behavior, or do we pick and choose our models?

Social learning theory states that we learn what we should do from the behavior of others, and are particularly inclined to learn from others who have some significance to us, who we see as our role models, and who we wish to reflect in our behavior. We give more weight to the behavior of role models, following it more closely, storing it better in our brains, and recalling it more easily. Role models therefore make more of a mark on our behavior than others within or outside our group. Kees Keizer (see also Chapters 14 and 15) shows the effect of this in a simple experiment. This is the final flyer experiment to be discussed in this book.

Keizer fixed a flyer advertising the latest issue of the magazine *Knowledge* to the handlebars of a number of bicycles in the bike shed of a university. On the flyer was the text: "The majority of ..., 80 percent, commit plagiarism. Read all about it in *Knowledge*." One set of flyers stated that 80 percent of professors committed plagiarism. Next to the text was a photo of a professor in a toga. On the other flyers the text stated that 80 percent of students committed plagiarism, with a photo of a student. In both photos a black strip was printed across the eyes, to emphasize that plagiarism was a transgression of the norm. Once again there was no trash can to be seen in the area. What did they discover? Of the cyclists who found the flyer with the student, 39 percent threw it on the ground. The flyer with the professor was thrown away a third more, at 52 percent.

Those who symbolize group norms are more influential in determining the behavior of people in that group than are other group members. In Keizer's experiment the professors were the role models for the students, so that the reprehensible behavior of the professors had more influence on the behavior of students throwing away flyers than that of their fellow students. In organizations, directors, managers, and leaders are important role models for the behavior of others within and around the organization. They are expected to represent the norms of the organization. The higher they are in the organization the more this applies.

My own research shows that in organizations where the management sets a good example, significantly less unethical behavior is seen in the rest of the organization than when the management sets a bad example. Thirty-two aspects of unethical behavior were measured, including actions such as cheating consumers, squeezing out suppliers, deceiving shareholders, competing unfairly, and violating human rights. At the same time employees and outsiders are often critical of the lack of role-modeling at the top. The positive side of this criticism is that it conceals an expectation: employees and outsiders expect top management to give a good example. That means that there is a need for ethical leadership. But what exactly is ethical leadership?

First of all, ethical leaders have a moral compass. They explore their environment, with a well-developed vision of right and wrong. They have a clear sense of direction when it comes to deciding what can and must be done better. They see and hear what others do not see or hear. They not only draw a clear line between what is and what is not permissible, but at the same time push the boundaries, and raise the bar, for others as well as themselves to become more ethical.

Ethical leaders have courage. They not only know that things must and can be different, but they *do* things differently themselves. They don't flow downstream like dead fish, they swim against the current. A head wind makes them strong, causing them to rise like a kite. They have the drive and the guts to persist where others give up. Where others are silent, they speak. They demand responsibility. As American president Obama said, in response to criticism of greed in the financial sector, "Ultimately, I'm responsible. The buck stops with me. And my goal is to make sure that we never put ourselves in this kind of position again."

The director of a consultancy in Florida gave an unusual example of courage. Due to the recession 51-year-old Lol Gonzalez was forced to make one of her employees redundant. Instead she herself decided to leave. "How can you sack someone who trusted you and who you trusted too?" she said when the news came out. The staff were astonished when she actually began to clear her desk. "They thought I'd gone mad," said Gonzalez. This may be characteristic of ethical leadership; letting others initially think you have gone mad. Fortunately the staff did not take this model behavior literally by following suit and resigning; instead they became more motivated in their work for the consultancy firm.

Ethical behavior is not only for people in management positions. Ultimately ethical leadership should show people that they are not the product of their environment, but are capable of creating an environment in which they can get the best out of themselves and others. Are you such a leader?

18 Morals Melt Under Pressure: Authority and Obedience

Organizations operate on the basis of power and authority. The employees must do the management's bidding. Once something is decided by the management, it must be carried out by subordinates. When push comes to shove the boss has the final say. This obedience is instilled in us from birth: parents know what is good for us, teachers tell us what we need to know. If everyone did their own thing, it would be chaos. How obedient are people?

Do they remain obedient when this requires them to ride roughshod over others? What does this mean for work?

Imagine you work as a nurse in a hospital. One day you receive a phone call from a doctor you do not know. He asks you to administer medicine to a patient immediately, so that it has taken effect by the time he arrives. He will sign the request for the medicine, which is unfamiliar to you, on arrival. The doctor tells you that the patient must receive 20 milligrams of the medicine. You walk to the medicine cabinet and take out the medicine. On the label you read that a dose of 5 milligrams is normal and 10 milligrams is the absolute maximum. You return to the telephone. What do you say to the doctor?

Charles Hofling and his colleagues put this hypothetical dilemma to nurses in their research. Eighty-three percent said they would not follow the doctor's request. But what happened when the researchers actually phoned a hospital and followed the script described above? Only 5 percent of nurses refused to administer the double dose. The rest followed the request, if rather hesitantly in some cases. Luckily the medicine was a placebo, so, unbeknown to the nurses, the patient was in no danger.

An important theme in social psychology is obedience to authority, in this case the nurse's obedience to the doctor, but it could equally be employee to manager, manager to director, director to chairman of the board, or chairman of the board to governors, shareholders, and regulators. How far will people take obedience? In the example above, nurses could still assume that if the doctor said it, the overdose would not be harmful to the patient. But what do people do if the results are indisputably damaging, if they can see with their own eyes that it is wrong?

Stanley Milgram carried out a famous experiment in the 1960s, at the time of the case against the war criminal Adolf Eichmann. Milgram wanted to know if war criminals had a common morality. Did they share certain character traits or was it the situation that made them as they were? Milgram therefore carried out the following experiment.

The subjects were asked to take part in memory research. The aim was to look into the effect of punishment on people's ability to learn. Observed by the researcher, dressed in a white laboratory jacket, two participants drew lots to determine who was the teacher and who was the student. The researcher then tied the student down on a chair and fastened an electrode to their wrist. The researcher smeared gel on the student's wrist and casually remarked that this would prevent any heavy shocks causing lasting tissue damage. The researcher and teacher then went into the adjoining room, where there was a machine. The student must now answer questions. For every wrong answer the teacher must administer a shock, increasing by 15 volts each time, to a maximum of 450 volts. The switches were labeled as follows: "shock," "moderate shock," "strong shock," "very strong shock," "intense shock," "extreme intensity shock," and "danger: severe shock." The final two switches were labeled with "XXX (=death)." In order to show that the device worked, the teacher was given a shock of 45 volts by the researcher as an example. Ouch!

What the teacher did not know, was that he was the only subject of research and that the student in the plot was always the same person (a much used trick in such experiments). Luckily no actual shocks were administered, but the teacher only discovered this afterwards. During the experiment the teacher could not see the student, but could hear him. In reality a tape was played, adjusted according the strength of the shocks administered: for light shocks faint sobbing could be heard. Gradually the cries increased, as did heated requests to stop ("Let me go, let me go!"). From 300 volts banging on the wall could be heard, followed by a deathly scream. After this the student was unresponsive and there was dead silence. The teacher was told by the researcher that this should be taken as a wrong answer and the next switch should be used. In the case that the teacher hesitated or asked for advice, the researcher gave one of the four standardized incitements, which were strict, self-confident, and devoid of emotion: at the first sign of doubt the researcher said, "Please go on"; at the second he said, "The experiment requires you to continue"; at the third, "It is absolutely essential that you continue"; and at the fourth, "You have no other choice, you *must* go on." If the subject refused after the fourth incitement, then the experiment ended. This also happened if the teacher gave someone the highest shock (450 volts).

Milgram was curious as to how fast people would drop out. What did he discover? The subjects persisted to an average of 360 volts, and almost two-thirds administered the highest and deadly shock of 450 volts. Many people refused to believe these results, so the research has been repeated many times, always with approximately the same results.

According to Milgram, the results show that "the essence of obedience consists in the fact that a person comes to view themselves as the instrument for carrying out another person's wishes, and they therefore no longer see themselves as responsible for their actions." According to Milgram this meant that *Befehl ist Befehl* ("an order is an order") was not something typically German (as was hoped at the time, as an explanation for the Second World War), but that almost everyone is obedient in certain circumstances and participates in reprehensible, disgraceful acts. According to Milgram perfectly ordinary people can be middlemen in a destructive course of events. Even when the effects of their behavior are clear, relatively few people have the strength to resist authority if they are asked to continue. Under the pressure of authority people's morals melt away.

The aura of authority was enforced in this experiment by a number of factors: the researcher was attached to a renowned university, wore a white lab coat, and talked in a self-confident tone. In organizations people gain authority through factors such as experience, age, income, status, education, communication skills, clothing and jewelry, and the size and interior design of their office. Although authority can be positive, it is important to keep an eye out for negative side effects. A leadership position encourages people to follow. Wherever there is leadership there will be people who follow. Asking others to do something means that they are less inclined to feel responsible for the execution and consequences, because they are not responsible for the request and can hide behind their leader. In this respect managers cannot overestimate their power to influence subordinates.

If you have power and authority, it is obviously morally unacceptable to abuse this power by asking others to do morally unacceptable things. Unfortunately it is not always so obvious. Approximately a third of the American professional population admits that their manager sometimes asks them to do unethical or illegal things.

So if you are in a position of authority and ask something of someone, be aware that people will not necessarily only do things they agree with and see as ethically responsible. One might protest, but another will make the mental switch and do what is asked of him. In Milgram's experiment people could relatively easily leave; in an organization this is considerably more difficult. Yet the participants of the experiment still went a long way in causing human suffering. How easy must it be to grant requests involving misdemeanors such as fraud, theft, and scams, which have less human suffering as a consequence?

One way of steeling yourself against carrying out and submitting to improper requests is not to see responsibility as a fixed quantity. With responsibility it does not necessarily hold that the more one person is responsible, the less responsibility another bears. When one person asks another to do something and the other complies, the sum of responsibilities increases. If you do something because another person tells you to, you are still responsible for the decision to comply with the request. Shirking responsibility is by definition irresponsible, because you are then unable to explain why you acted as you did. It is therefore important not to follow dubious orders unthinkingly, but to raise questions.

There was a small ray of hope: it was not without emotion that Milgram's subjects administered the shocks. Every participant paused at least once and questioned what was going on. They followed this up with protests, head-shaking, sweating, nervousness, stammering, trembling, lip-biting, and digging their nails into their arms. More than a third began to laugh nervously. People breathed a sigh of relief when the experiment ended, wiped their foreheads dry, and shook their heads in regret. That suggested that their conscience was speaking.

19 Trapped in the Role: Clothes Make the Man

Power dressing is a powerful tool. That is the conclusion of Stefanie Tzioti's PhD thesis. Her empirical research shows that a consultant's advice is more readily followed when the consultant has a suit and a car of the right brand. Dressing to impress increases authority in the eyes of the customer and therefore the credibility of the advice.

We also saw this effect in Milgram's experiment (described in the previous chapter). The researcher's white jacket gave the impression of expertise and authority, making the participants more inclined to follow the order to administer electric shocks. Clothing can have all kinds of surprising effects at work as well: research by Dan Ariely shows that provocatively dressed women make men think more in the short term. For a meeting about long-term policy female personnel are best advised to dress demurely.

Clothing not only determines how someone is seen, it also betrays the way in which the wearer sees himself. As Princess Perdita in Shakespeare's *The Winter's Tale* says, "This robe of mine does change my disposition." Scott Fraser demonstrates the speed with which clothing can change attitudes.

He had children choose what kind of game they wanted to play. Wearing their own clothes, 42 percent chose aggressive games, but when the researcher had them wear a military uniform, the choice for aggressive games increased to 86 percent. When the children subsequently exchanged their uniforms for their own clothing again, the percentage fell, even dropping below the original reading, to 36 percent.

Clothing can be a reflection of one's role, and we easily fall into that role. On the one hand this is positive; it shows a good ability to empathize and adapt. On the other hand it can be risky. We can lose ourselves in a role. This is shown by Philip Zimbardo, who conducted a controversial experiment in the cellars of Stanford University in 1971.

A group of 24 mainly white middle-class American youths participated in a two-week role play in a pretend prison, created by Zimbardo in the cellars of the university. The students did not have a criminal record and were found to be "normal" according to a psychological test carried out beforehand. Half of the participants (randomly chosen by tossing a coin) were given a khaki uniform, a whistle, a police baton, and reflective sunglasses. Their task was to keep order in the prison without resorting to violence. They must base their actions on a set of 16 rules. The "prisoners" (the other half of the group) were only permitted to eat during mealtimes, and must always address the guards as "Mr. Correctional Officer" and one another by their identification numbers. Anyone who violated the rules was to be subjected to punishment, to be determined by the guards themselves. The prisoners had their heads shaved, were required to strip off all their clothes, and received prison uniforms with their identification numbers printed on them and a pair of rubber sandals. They were chained by their ankles. Zimbardo and his colleagues were curious as to what would happen in this setting.

During the first day everything went according to plan. On the second morning, however, a rebellion broke out. The prisoners wanted to test the system: they tore their identification numbers off their uniforms, barricaded the door with their beds, and challenged the guards by insulting them. After consultation, the guards decided to tackle the rebellion heavy-handedly. The doors were forced with a fire extinguisher, the rebels were made to take off their clothes, the beds were removed, and the leader of the rebellion was locked in the isolation cell. This was just the beginning.

As time passed the guards became increasingly sadistic and the prisoners more submissive and depressive. The prisoners were forced to carry out pointless tasks: continually chanting the rules or performing sexual acts. The guards also threatened the prisoners with physical violence. After just two days, five of the prisoners (almost half!) fell into an extreme state of depression, continually crying, and exhibiting fits of rage and panic attacks. One prisoner developed a psychosomatic skin condition. The guards began to carry out their abuses at night, because they thought the researchers were not looking then. Most guards felt good about their task. Some even took pleasure in treating the prisoners cruelly. No one said that this could not continue.

It was not only the subjects who lost themselves in the experiment: the team of 50 researchers fell into their own trap. They observed everything carefully and did not stop to ask themselves whether the experiment could continue. Zimbardo himself said afterwards that he felt himself transform into the governor of the prison, more interested in order in the prison than the well-being of the participants. Only when an outsider came by to do some interviews, and wondered why the prisoners were walking around with bags over their heads and were led to the toilet with their ankles chained were Zimbardo's eyes opened and did he grasp the fact that things had gone wrong. After 6 of the planned 14 days, the experiment was brought to a halt, much to the surprise of the guards.

The experiment shows the dramatic effects of placing normal people in different roles: they reached that point of changed and degrading behavior in a space of six days, and all of this in a fake prison. The psychological explanation for the behavior of guards, prisoners, and researchers is that they completely internalized the roles assigned to them, and in doing so adopted the norms implicit in these roles. The stereotypes suggested that guards must be authoritarian, and prisoners submissive. As in Milgram's experiment, blind obedience was at issue, determined by the image people had of their role. After a few days both the prisoners and the guards had forgotten that they were participating in an experiment. It felt *real*. Their own identity had been erased. The prisoners had become numbers and the guards had become "Mr. Correctional Officer." Although they knew that this was an experiment, the expectations associated with the roles were sufficiently powerful and overwhelming to pull the participants into the scenario completely. They were prisoners of their own roles.

The natural initial question is what type of guard you would be if you were placed in this experiment. Zimbardo, however, saw this as irrelevant, because most people adapted to the situation and let themselves go, even if they claimed beforehand that they would always remain true to themselves. Another, more relevant question is what role you are assigned, which norms you ascribe to it, and whether these norms are acceptable. If you are a salesperson, do you consider it desirable to be opportunistic, insistent, or even aggressive, and to be flexible with the truth? If you are a civil servant, do you consider it normal to be loyal and obedient to the government in all matters? If you are a politician, do you consider it a moral obligation to be hypocrite, to lie, and to be feared? If you are a manager or director, do you consider it praiseworthy to squeeze and exploit employees, to make them serve your needs, and listen to you in silence?

Adopting a role can also work positively. Roles can conjure up images which bring out the best in people. As a salesperson you can also improve the well-being of your customers, respect their autonomy, and be open and honest. As a politician you can serve the interests of society, be aware of different interests, and justify the trust bestowed on you. As a manager or director you can aim to help others excel, subordinate yourself to this goal, and listen to what others expect of you. So it comes all down to how roles are perceived and whether someone is the prisoner of his own role, or the guard.

20 Power Corrupts, But Not Always: Hypocrisy and Hypercrisy

The media regularly reports on the crooked dealings of influential people: the singer who preaches family values, while involved in an extramarital affair, the director who reduces his staff's salaries and doubles his own bonus, the police commissioner who is strict in tackling speeding, but floors the gas pedal in a built-up area, and the politician who speaks out for honest government, but allows himself to be bribed by business. One explanation often offered is that everyone occasionally oversteps the mark, even those in high positions. The only difference is that the behavior of people in high places receives more public attention: tall trees catch the most wind.

Another possible reason is that people in high places are expected to have higher moral standards and therefore fail more readily and significantly. An employee of a random company who fiddles his private tax return will not be sacked, while a politician must pack up and leave for this.

There is another, additional explanation. Joris Lammers and colleagues questioned whether power in itself leads to a greater chance of unacceptable behavior. In order to test their suspicions, they carried out the following experiment. The participants were assigned a role in which they either had a great deal of power or very little. One participant, for example, would be a government minister, the other a civil servant. They were then asked to give their opinions on various unethical situations, varying from breaking speed limits in order to arrive at an appointment on time, not declaring private income to the tax authorities and taking possession of a stolen bicycle left in the street.

The results showed that the more power people have the more they condemn the unethical behavior of others. Speeding, for example, received 6.3 on a nine-point scale (from completely unacceptable to completely acceptable) from the participants with power, while the participants with little power gave it 7.3. At the same time it was shown that the more power people have the less they disapprove of their own unethical behavior. The powerful participants rated their own speeding at 7.6, and those with little power rated their own speeding at 7.2.

The research by Lammers and colleagues shows that the more powerful people are, the more hypocritical they become: they expect more of others and less of themselves. They set the bar higher for others and lower for themselves. For the less powerful participants the disparity between the judgment of their own behavior and that of others was only −0.1 (7.2 as compared to 7.3), whereas for the powerful participants the difference was +1.3 (7.6 compared to 6.3).

As shown in experiments described in previous chapters, this all comes down to the pictures (cognitive schemata) people have of power, influence, and standing. If people are set up as influential, then this activates schemata consistent with this. One specific schema is that influential people have the right to judge others, to maintain order and standards. Judges, police officers, and teachers are tasked with judging the behavior of others. Within organizations the management and supporting departments take on this task. With this responsibility people in influential positions are stricter in the judgment of others. That is one side of the coin. The other side is the schema that people in influential positions are more permissive toward themselves than those who are less influential. The more influence a person has, the more he places himself above others, such as his employees, in order to supervise their adherence to the rules. The management of the organization sets the rules which are carried out by employees and which the management again oversees. This feeds the image of the rules being less applicable to the influential person himself. After all, he does not belong to the party being supervised. Supervision requires distance. But by placing oneself above another party, one runs the risk of placing oneself above the legal and moral standards. That's also why people in influential positions become gradually less sensitive to what others think; after all, the others are different.

The more influence someone has, the more privileges they have. This prompts people to acquire more influence. Privileges already acquired are grasped with both hands, not only because they are seen as a reward (for the responsibilities they bear), but also because they form proof of increased influence. This reasoning can give rise to the feeling that the more influence one has, the more unique one becomes. Influence is, after all, a rare commodity. The more influence one has, the more exceptional one is, and the more one can permit oneself. As a chairman of the board of a financial institution said, "Few people can do what I can do, just like few people can do what Justine Henin can do." This chairman said this at the point when the tennis star Henin had topped the world rankings for 117 weeks. Pride, however, comes before a fall, and soon afterwards the chairman was forced to leave. His optimistic view of the share price had stirred up a great deal of ill feeling with the shareholders. Furthermore he had failed to pay out the promised dividend. He was even hypocritical enough to ask for a huge bonus for himself, in defiance of all procedures. And his golden parachute was in stark contrast to the great losses suffered by shareholders. All this prompted an association of securities holders to proclaim him the "biggest money grabber" in the country.

Does this mean that absolute power corrupts absolutely, as is often said? Follow-up research by Lammers and colleagues fortunately offers a corrective. When people are unconscious of their power or think their power is undeserved, the opposite appears to be the case: they judge their own behavior more strictly than the behavior of others. This phenomenon is known as "hypercrisy," a very critical judgment of oneself.

In order to avoid hypocrisy it is therefore important to think as little as possible of the power you have. Do not imagine that you stand above others, but rather under them: that is true servant leadership. Is that not exemplary role-modeling?

21 Beeping Bosses: Fear, Aggression, and Uncertainty

In the previous chapter we saw that people who feel powerful and influential more readily fall prey to double standards. Where else do power, influence, and prestige lead?

Imagine you are in the car on the way to an important appointment. It is essential that you arrive on time; you absolutely must not be late. It's going to be tight, but if the traffic lights are on your side then it should work out. Just as you think that, the car in front of you brakes suddenly because the traffic light jumps to red. It feels like forever, but eventually the traffic light turns green again. Just when you want to get moving you see that the car in front is staying still. You can't get by. What you can do is beep your horn. That way you can draw the driver's attention to the fact that the light is green and that you are waiting. Perhaps his mind is on other things or he cannot see the traffic light very well. It could also be that he is on the phone or eating or is simply an idiot who can't get moving. That's all you need when you're in a hurry! With a long, hard push on the horn you can make it clear that you do not appreciate this. Any idea what you would do?

Whether and how hard you beep depends on many factors: how much of a hurry you are in, why you think the car is not moving, and how short your fuse is, for example. According to Andreas Diekmann and colleagues this could also depend on your social status. They carried out an experiment to test this.

One afternoon two researchers stopped a middle-class car at a traffic light on a busy junction. When the light turned green they stayed still. The researchers then registered whether and how soon the driver of the car blocked behind them beeped. The researchers took this as a measure of aggression.

In all cases the car reacted: a quarter signaled with the headlights and three-quarters beeped. The average reaction time was 4.2 seconds, but this varied from 1.4 to 17 seconds. This big difference was not explained by the presence of fellow passengers, the age, or color of the blocked car, the gender of the driver, or the day of the week. The reaction time was partially affected by the age of the driver (the younger the driver, the faster they beeped), but this was not the main determining factor. What might predict the reaction time? The researchers looked at the class of the blocked car. According to the researchers this is symbolic of the driver's social position. The higher the class, the higher the status. This indeed turned out to affect reaction time: drivers of lower, cheaper class cars had an average response time of 5 seconds, while people with cars of a higher, more expensive class on average reacted within 2 seconds. The more luxurious the car, the faster people beeped. According to Diekmann and colleagues, their research proves that a higher social position leads to more aggression in traffic.

As far as I know, the issue of whether there is more aggression high up in the organization than lower down has not yet been researched. It does, however, appear that there is abundant aggression at the top of organizations where standards are low. Board members and managers intimidate personnel by snapping, being quick to go off at the deep end, and other hostile behavior. It is known that Bernie Ebbers, the CEO of WorldCom, the telecoms company that fell in 2000 due to one of the greatest cases of accounting fraud in history, was aggressive. He specialized in confrontational politics and publicly belittled employees. Dick Fuld, former CEO of Lehman Brothers, was also known for his aggression. His nickname was "the gorilla," because of his machismo and intimidating conduct.

Extending our interpretation of Diekmann and colleagues' research, we might assume that the higher the status of the boss, the more likely he is to "beep." This may be a show of power, but there may also be other reasons. Nathanael Fast and Serena Chen researched how people in a leadership position react to feelings of uncertainty as to their own suitability (which incidentally may be independent of their actual suitability). Participants were required to beep a horn whenever a "subordinate" gave a wrong answer to a question. They could choose from sounds varying from 10 to 130 decibels. Uncertain managers opted relatively frequently for a loud beep. The researchers suggest that the combination of great power and the feeling of unsuitability leads people to lash out at others.

It is therefore a case of watching out for loud beeping bosses, who are loud but have little to say.

22 Fare Dodgers and Black Sheep: When Model Behavior Backfires

A good example encourages good behavior, and a bad example, unfortunately, encourages bad behavior, as we have seen. However, these truths do not always apply; the opposite can also happen. Let us begin with a study that shows that model behavior by one person can lead to bad behavior by another.

For a change of scene, this study by Paul Webley and Claire Siviter looks at the behavior of dog walkers. The researchers hid in park woods and observed whether people cleaned up properly after their dogs. Leaving dog poop was explicitly prohibited in all study locations. After the dog and owner had continued their walk, one of the researchers approached them and asked the owner to participate in a study on the pros and cons of owning a dog. Filling in the survey would only take a few minutes. The survey included a few questions on the issue of whether or not people clean up after their dog and the reasons for this, the part that the researchers were really interested in.

Because the researchers had seen for themselves whether the participants cleaned up, they were able to form two groups and compare these. The non-cleaners were predominantly of the opinion that the law in this area was too strict ("Poop is biodegradable after all") and that there was too little room to let dogs off the lead. They turned out to estimate the amount of dog poop considerably lower than the group which did clean up after their dogs.

One group complying with the norm led to another group violating it. An explanation for this is that people consider it acceptable to violate a rule if they think that everyone else complies with it. In that case it's not so bad, the total damage is limited. This is known as the *free rider problem*: if I know that others do the right thing, then I can take liberties. This is the reason why it is often awkward to get rid of irregularities in an organization altogether: occasionally taking office stationary home can't do any harm, as long as your colleagues don't do it too. Occasionally breaking an environmental law is no problem, as long as other companies in the area behave properly. Of course it is a problem if everyone thinks this way.

Good behavior can therefore lead to bad behavior, but could the opposite also be the case? That bad behavior leads to good behavior? In order to study this, Francesca Gino and colleagues came up with the following experiment. The participants, students of the University of Pittsburgh, divided into groups of 8–14, were required to perform 20 tasks in which (as in the experiment described in Chapter 10) they must find two numbers on each page which added up to 10 precisely. They were given 5 minutes to do this. They were then allowed to determine their own score and take 50 cents out of an envelope placed on the table for them. The participants then put their answer sheets through a shredder, so that no one could find out whether they had cheated. One group served as a control; these participants were required to hand in their answers, so that the researchers could find out what the actual score was. But here is the crux. The researchers had placed an assistant in some groups. This participant, dressed in a white T-shirt, made it known very conspicuously that he was finished after 1 minute. He said that he had answered all the questions right and could take the 10 dollars home. For the other participants there was only one possible interpretation: this was a cheat. What effect would this have on the behavior of the other participants? Would they now also cheat?

In the control group, where no cheating was possible, seven questions were answered correctly, so the participants received 3.5 dollars. In the groups without an assistant, the participants on average claimed to have answered 12 questions correctly. The average cheat therefore lied about five questions. In the groups with an assistant, the participants on average claimed to have answered 15 questions correctly: more than double the score of the group which could not cheat. This illustrates the effect of a rotten apple on the behavior in the group. The notion that this person belonged *in* the group was indeed the relevant point. What happened when the assistant, instead of wearing a white T-shirt, wore a T-shirt with the logo of Carnegie Mellon University, the arch rival of the University of Pittsburgh? The participants now claimed to have answered eight questions correctly, considerably less than in the situation in which the cheat was seen as a student from the same university, and even considerably less than when there was no cheat in the group!

Gino and colleagues' experiment shows that when the rotten apple is seen as belonging to their group it "infects" the other apples. When the rotten apple is seen as a rival, an outsider, the cheating decreases, as if it has had a cleansing effect. People distance themselves from the reprehensible behavior of "the other" ("We're not like that, we *don't want* to be like that"). The reprehensible behavior activates an awareness of the difference in norms between the two groups and strengthens the awareness of norms in one's own group. It acts as a motivation to do better. This was also seen by Cialdini and colleagues in their research, described in Chapter 14: when someone passed by in a clean environment and did nothing, 14 percent of the visitors threw their flyer on the ground, but when the passer-by himself threw a flyer on the ground the percentage did not increase, but in fact dropped to 6 percent.

One black sheep will not necessarily attract followers: a sheep from another flock will not be followed. And if a sheep from one's own flock behaves badly, then it is possible to prevent the example being followed by labeling him a black sheep. Dissidents are not necessarily a serious problem. They may even improve the behavior of others.

Factor 3: Achievability

In the previous section we explored the importance of role-modeling. Whether they like it or not, it is the attitude and behavior of managers that to a large extent determines the ethics and integrity of organizations. It is essential that managers are aware of their key role, not only because of their model function, but also because of their susceptibility to undesirable behavior.

In addition to role-modeling, there is a third factor which affects behavior in organizations. This factor is "achievability." It is not only a matter of people knowing what they *should* do, but also that they *can* do it. Achievability relates to the freedom and opportunities people have to realize their goals, duties, and responsibilities.

The following nine chapters discuss experiments illustrating the meaning of achievability. The way goals are set affects people's behavior. Goals can be one-sided, leading to tunnel vision, as shown in Chapter 23. They can also result in wastefulness, if they are seen as a ceiling, as described in Chapter 24. They may lead to perilous situations, if only one person can achieve the goal and the rest have no chance of it, as discussed in Chapter 25, or if the aims are set too high, as explained in Chapter 26.

Achievability also relates to the power people have to fulfill what is expected of them. In Chapter 27 we therefore discuss the importance of persistence, while in Chapter 28 the importance of implementation plans is raised. Once a person has started on one course of action, desirable behavior can become unfeasible, as there is no longer any way back. In Chapter 29 we see how people can end up on a slippery slope, while in Chapter 30 three techniques are presented for tricking people into taking a certain decision or course of action. Finally in Chapter 31 we see how the feeling of lacking room for maneuver can lead to undesirable behavior.

23 Goals and Blinkers: Tunnel Vision and Teleopathy

Management is about realizing goals. Leadership, in contrast, is primarily about setting the right goals. Goals are therefore essential both to management and to leadership: without goals, concepts such as "effectiveness" (progress toward a goal) and "efficiency" (proportionality of effort to the goal) are meaningless. Hundreds of scientific studies have shown that setting goals, especially challenging, specific and measurable goals, has a positive effect on people's effort, persistence, and achievements. Achieving goals is psychologically rewarding, in terms of better self-esteem and higher levels of satisfaction.

In striving for a goal, however, there is also a hidden danger: tunnel vision. The focus on a goal then becomes a fixation, and other important things fall by the wayside. Just as with tunnel vision, people focus on the light at the end; the rest is dark, does not count, and is not seen. The field of vision narrows and everything else is made subordinate to that one goal. This can lead to irrational behavior. Research suggests, for example, that only 15 percent of disaster victims continue to think calmly and rationally. Tunnel vision can also lead to unethical behavior.

A typical example of tunnel vision is the parable of the Sadhu. An expedition of businessmen on their way up a mountain in the Himalayas came across an Indian man. This Sadhu was very sick and barely clothed. Without help he would die. After internal consultation the expedition decided not to help the man and to continue their climb. The expedition members felt that they had no time to lose. They simply had to reach the top. In their eyes it was now or never. A great deal of money had gone into the preparation of this climb. Only the top of the mountain counted.

Tunnel vision happens within organizations too. A classic example is the production of the Ford Pinto. In the 1960s the Ford Motor Company set itself the goal of producing a car for less than 2,000 dollars by 1970. An ambitious, concrete, and measurable goal. Nice! However, in order to reach this goal the results of some safety tests were ignored and the Ford Pinto was introduced to the market with an increased risk of explosion upon rear-end collision. The sad consequence was that a total of 53 people were killed due to this narrow vision. Tunnel vision also occurred at Enron. The employees received large bonuses for the trade they brought in. This made them so focused on their sales that they no longer looked at whether these were profitable. The enterprise, with its good sales figures (and large bonuses), headed into the financial abyss.

Tunnel vision is a dangerous phenomenon. When particular goals dominate, unscrupulous behavior may go unnoticed: the end justifies the means. We see tunnel vision in the organization that must grow at any cost and makes everything subordinate to that goal, and in the employee who wants to get ahead, and sacrifices everything else, even his private life, for it. Tunnel vision can also occur in private life: hobbies which get out of hand, love which turns into obsession, frugality which degenerates into meanness, and patriotism which leads to nationalism and fundamentalism.

Tunnel vision is a common phenomenon within organizations, also called "teleopathy" in the literature (after the Greek words "goal" and "sickness"). Goal sickness is obsession with goals. The only thing that counts is the goal. Not achieving it is disastrous.

In a simple experiment, Barry Staw and Richard Boettger show how focusing on one goal leads to other issues being ignored or going unseen. They asked participating students to correct a proof containing prominent grammatical and content errors. The brochure text would be used as promotional material for a course in management. When the students were asked to correct as many grammatical errors as possible, they did not find any content errors, and vice versa. Only when the students were asked to do their very best to correct the brochure did they find both grammatical and content errors.

Another well-known experiment is that of Daniel Simons and Christopher Chabris. The participants were shown a video of two teams playing basketball. The participants were asked to count the number of times the team members passed the ball to one another. However, something crazy happens in the video: after 35 seconds a woman appears in the picture wearing a gorilla suit. She walks to the middle of the court, turns to the camera, beats her breast, and walks away again. Not something you would expect to miss. The players, meanwhile, continue with their game. Only half of the participants in the experiment noticed the gorilla. The other half were so busy counting that they failed to see the unexpected, even though it was clearly visible. Simons and Chabris call this "inattentional blindness."

There is always a danger of tunnel vision, but luckily it can be suppressed, by continuing to ask critical questions about how the goal relates to other goals and interests. What are the higher and underlying goals, for example? It is important to examine both the goal and the path to achieving it. Are the means justified?

Another important point is not to go too far in setting goals: often organizations are bursting at the seams with score cards, management contracts, job profiles, and assessment sheets. Setting more goals is not necessarily better. The opposite may be true: the more goals, the less they say. If people are pulled in all directions, then they will lose their way. Large numbers of goals create the impression that no clear choices have been made. Employees will tend to pick and choose the goals that they consider most important or focus on what they are already good at. Arbitrariness is the likely outcome. This has also been shown by research: when there are multiple goals, people focus on one, tending especially toward those which are easiest to achieve or to measure.

Setting the right goals and placing them in the right context is a real challenge. That's why it is rightly at the heart of management and leadership.

24 Own Goals: Seeing Goals as the Ceiling

The advantage of goals is that they give direction and impetus, but what happens once the goals have been achieved? Follow through and push on or pack up and go? Research by Colin Camerer and colleagues shows what taxi drivers in New York thought about this and what we can learn from it.

For years people wondered why it was so difficult to get a taxi on a rainy day in New York. The most obvious explanation was that demand was higher; more people take a taxi when it's raining than when it's dry. Camerer and colleagues, however, suspected that this was not the only reason. At the end of the 1990s they therefore decided to do a study. They discovered another contributing factor: the supply side was just as guilty. What was going on? When it rained, more taxis disappeared from the streets in the course of the day than when it was dry. Asking around among the taxi drivers, they traced this back to the goal that they set themselves: earning double what the taxi cost them per day. On rainy days they earned their money faster because the demand was indeed higher. They therefore reached their goal quicker and could go home early.

These results are at odds with the economic principle of income elasticity, which states that people work more if they can earn more and less when earnings are less. The goal the taxi drivers had set themselves was holding them back. If they were to set their goal differently, not per day but per month or per year, then the taxi drivers would be able both to earn more, by working more hours on rainy days than on sunny days instead of the other way round, and they would also not need to spend as much time at work. This would also benefit the drenched New Yorkers.

If a goal is seen as an end point, people stop when they achieve it. The product developer who has reached the set number of innovations for the year and rests on his laurels and the purchaser who achieves the budget reduction ahead of time and forgets to negotiate prices sharply for the rest of the year are both guilty of this. Organizations encourage this kind of behavior when exceeding goals is not shown extra appreciation, or even goes unrewarded. Sometimes it is actually indirectly punished, because the achievements of the current period are taken as minimal goals for the following period. Exceeding the goal now only means that more must be produced in the next period. Exceeding expectations can then be seen as shooting oneself in the foot.

To prevent this effect, some organizations decide to set goals so high that they can never be achieved. These companies then run the risk of achieving the opposite. The disadvantage of unachievable and unrealistic goals is that they can lead to lower motivation and effort. The theory of "perceived behavioral control" states that motivation and effort are influenced by the ease with which people think they can do something. If something seems easy, people have a great deal of motivation and put in a great deal of effort. If people expect it to be difficult, motivation and effort are reduced. People feel less in control of the situation, are less certain and committed, and more readily devote their effort to other things, such as taking precautions in case the goals are not achieved, which again takes up time which cannot be put toward achieving the goal itself. There is a very real risk of a self-fulfilling prophecy.

In other cases unrealistic goals are embraced precisely *because* they are unrealistic. Achievability then becomes a question of belief, characterized by a lack of evidence. Belief that the unbelievable can be achieved encourages a feeling of supremacy. People think that they can do anything and control everything, that the sky's the limit. Scandal and transgression are bound to follow such thoughts. Research from the beginning of this century shows companies involved in fraud stating growth figures two and a half times higher than those of honest companies. The more ambitious the goals, the higher the risk of dishonest behavior.

Richard Larrick and colleagues also researched whether specific and challenging goals led to more risky behavior than vaguer, less challenging goals. In their experiment two participants were required to come to an agreement over sharing out a moneybox containing eight chips. In order to minimize the effect of social factors, participants were not permitted to speak to one another. They were required to make their bid in writing and exchange offers simultaneously. In the first round every chip stood for 1 dollar, but in every round in which the participants failed to come to an agreement, the value dropped by 5 cents. If the total offer was lower or the same as the value of the eight chips, people were considered to have reached an agreement and the chips were paid out. If no agreement had been reached after five rounds, neither participant would receive anything. In principle the participants would benefit from bidding for as much as possible, so as to be able to cash more money. However, this was a risky strategy, because if both players thought this way an agreement would be reached too late, leading to a reduction in value or no win at all. Larrick and colleagues divided the participants into two groups. Participants of one group were asked to do their best and earn as much money as possible. Participants of the other group were instructed to set an ambitious and concrete sum as a goal, the average coming to 5.42 dollars.

Of the group who were required to do their best, only 12 percent employed the risky strategy of asking for more than half. This led to 78 percent coming to an agreement in the first round, and after three rounds 100 percent had agreed. Among the participants with a concrete and ambitious goal things went differently. In this group, 34 percent employed a risky strategy in the first round, and only 52 percent reached an agreement in this round. After five rounds this had increased to 82 percent. According to the researchers, setting ambitious, concrete goals leads to more risky behavior, and to a greater chance of participants going home empty-handed. The challenge is to set challenging goals without going to extremes.

An energy company tackled this challenge successfully: the teams were permitted to set their own achievement measures and targets. The subsequent goals were set 10−20 percent higher than the old, centrally decided targets, and they were achieved. Levels of satisfaction among employees *and* customers also rose sharply.

Another way of looking at things can also be successful; the trick is to see goals as the floor rather than the ceiling. The goal is the floor of the next level, a transitional phase instead of an end point. Realizing the goal provides a point when one can enjoy the achievement and look back in satisfaction, which is psychologically important. At the same time, this is the moment to look forward at how the capacities, talents, and remaining time can be used to reach a new and higher goal. In this way people climb what Minjung Koo and Ayelet Fishbach call the "goal ladder." With a series of progressive goals people and organizations can reach greater heights without falling more than one step.

25 The Winner Takes it All: Losing Your Way in the Maze of Competition

Competition is good, both within organizations and outside. It encourages innovation, increases efficiency, advances entrepreneurship, and rewards effort. There is often only one winner. Only one person can be the first, the biggest or the best, the one to land the job, fill the vacancy, or obtain the patent. The rest go empty-handed. As Abba once sang, "The Winner Takes It All." But is such competition always a good thing? Christiane Schwieren and Doris Weichselbaumer were curious as to whether competition for a single prize really leads to better achievements and what possible side effects would emerge. They came up with the following experiment.

Participants were required to solve as many mazes as possible on a computer in half an hour by moving the cursor from the starting point along the path to the end. In the non-competitive situation every participant, in addition to 3 dollars for participation, received 30 cents for every maze solved. In the competitive situation every participant received 3 dollars for participation, as before, and the one to solve the most mazes additionally received the money that he and the other five participants had won put together. The rest ended up with nothing more.

The participants were required to indicate how many mazes they had solved themselves. What were the results? In both scenarios 28 mazes were solved. In this respect competition did not affect performance. In fact it led to worse performance, which was revealed because the researchers paid attention to something different.

What the participants did not know, was that the computer kept track of the real score. This allowed the researchers to determine the extent of cheating for each participant. In the non-competitive situation, participants cheated by 1.3 mazes on average. In the competitive situation this was more than double, at 2.9 mazes. The participants in the competitive situation had also made more use of various prohibited options in the program, such as lowering the difficulty level and the use of a function which showed when the wrong path was chosen, to solve the maze quicker.

According to the researchers, instead of prompting the participants to do their best to achieve, the competition encouraged them to cheat. This meant that on balance performance deteriorated. The same can be seen in practice. People are so busy enhancing performance figures and other forms of fraud that time and attention are diverted from the original goal. This leads to deterioration in actual performance. In short, the more one is concerned with enhancing the figures, the more likely it is that the figures will need enhancing.

What also struck the researchers was that female participants cheated more than male participants. This was remarkable because a large body of research suggests that women are more, not less, ethical. Moreover it appeared that female participants on average reported lower scores than male participants. This, too, is remarkable. If you cheat, then at least do it properly. The researchers looked for an explanation. They calculated the relationship between the number of mazes each participant had actually solved and the number of mazes reported which had not been solved. This showed that the skilled participants, those who had really solved relatively many mazes, cheated just as much in the competitive situation as in the non-competitive situation. That is, on average 1 maze per participant. Cheating was especially prevalent among the participants who were less skilled in solving the mazes. In the non-competitive situation the number of unfairly claimed mazes came to almost 2, while in the competitive situation the figure was almost 5. This explained the prevalence of cheating among female participants. The female participants were not more inclined to cheat *per se*. They were less skilled in solving mazes and that's why they cheated more.

The experiment reveals a dark side to competition. Situations in which there is one winner and the rest are losers encourage cheating. Those with less chance of winning are more inclined to cheat. After all, they have nothing to lose, or will do anything to avoid losing face. They therefore have the greatest chance of losing their integrity and getting lost in the maze of competition.

However, it is not the case that people with the least chance of winning are always the most inclined to lie and cheat. Experimental research by Maurice Schweitzer and colleagues shows that people are most likely to cheat when they are just short of their goal. The smaller the gap, the smaller the transgression, and the less that weighs against the reward of achieving the goal anyway. Moreover the smaller the gap, the more easily it can be closed with the argument that one might just as easily have actually achieved the goal or that the target could just as easily have been a little lower.

It is therefore important to be wary of situations in which there is only one winner. They lead to use of drugs in sport, plagiarism in science, beefed up CVs, bribery over tenders, inflated profits, and glossed-over losses. If there can only be one winner, the players are more inclined to want to win at any price. If everyone thinks this way, ethics and integrity are compromised. A race to the bottom is set in motion. But there's no need to throw the baby out with the bathwater. Competition can have a positive effect, as long as it gives direction and impetus. It is a good idea to apply a gradual reward curve. A system with progressive goals works best. If a salesperson earns a nice trip abroad for selling 100 cars, he must also receive something if he sells 99, otherwise it's like leaving the cat to guard the cream. Perhaps instead of giving one salesperson an exotic trip it would be better to do something with all the salespeople for the same money.

Don't take the refrain from "The Winner Takes It All" too seriously. Abba sings: "The winner takes it all. The loser has to fall. It's simple and it's plain. Why should I complain?" This might apply in love, but if the winner takes all in work and the rest get nothing, then it's time to address the issue.

26 From Jerusalem to Jericho: Time Pressure and Slack

Work pressure is high in many organizations. Some people need this pressure and seek it out. They can only achieve under pressure. That's when they get the most out of themselves and achieve *flow*, losing themselves in their work. Some just can't sit still; without time pressure they become impatient or start misbehaving due to boredom. Others see time as a gift that must be usefully employed.

There are pros to time pressure. An experiment by John Darley and Daniel Batson illustrates that there are also cons. The subjects were theology students who were assigned the task of giving a short sermon about the Bible story of the good Samaritan. In this story a Jewish man on his way from Jerusalem to Jericho is attacked by robbers and abandoned. Various role models who stood for piety at the time, such as a priest and a Levite, saw the man lying there but passed him without helping. Then a Samaritan came along. Although Jews were the enemies of the Samaritans, the Samaritan cared for the Jewish man and brought him to a hostel, where he paid for his stay. The theme of the sermon was "helpfulness." After the students were finished with their preparations they were told that the sermon would be filmed in another building on the university campus. The theology instructor gave them directions. On the way to the other building they passed a man who needed help. This man, who was part of the researchers' plan, appeared to have collapsed in the doorway. His head was bowed and his eyes were closed. At the moment that the student passed him, he gave a well-practiced groan and coughed twice. Would the theology students help the man?

When the theology students received plenty of time to walk to the other building, they almost all helped the man, but when the researchers ensured that the students set off late, the proportion prepared to help fell to 63 percent. More than a third of the students did not stop for the man. But here's the real shock. When the instructor encouraged the students to get to the other building as fast as possible, because there was no time to lose, the percentage plummeted, only 10 percent still stopping to help. Of the theology students on their way to preach about helpfulness, 90 percent ignored a man in need of help. Some students even stepped over him.

Despite the best of intentions, under time pressure we can still end up ignoring people who need our help. We no longer even see that others need us. After all, we are busy doing important things. Time pressure causes moral blindness: we shut down our senses partially or completely, even as we preach that it is important to help others. Time pressure can also lead to tasks not being carried out well or being rushed. This leads us to make mistakes more easily. Because of pressure to get to the other side as quickly as possible, staff on *The Herald of Free Enterprise* failed to properly follow safety instructions and the boat capsized just after leaving the Belgian port of Zeebrugge in 1987, drowning 193 people.

What can be done about this? First we must rid ourselves of the idea that pressure is definitively positive. People may well like to be seen as the busy boss, but instead of measuring effort in overtime, it would be better to value those who have time to spare. A chairman of the board of a large telecoms company was not ashamed to say that he played golf at least once a week during working hours to relax. He also said that he never felt that he had to work hard. Fortunately concepts such as "slow life," "slow management," and "slow food," placing the emphasis on slowing down and enjoying a higher quality of life and work, are winning ground.

A second method is to avoid seeing time pressure as a given. You don't *have* time, you *make* time, as they say. The same goes for time pressure, not so much because people *must* do a great deal, but from the fact that people *want* to do a great deal and cannot cope with it. Time pressure not only suggests that the organization has set the goals too high, but also that there is insufficient capacity and quality to realize these goals. It is, after all, the gap between obligation and ability which creates work and time pressure.

A third remedy for too much time pressure is creating slack. Slack is leeway, or useful redundancy. There is then time to accommodate unexpected interruptions, disappointments, and delays and to develop new things. At some companies employees have the option of doing "nothing" for 20 percent of their time. That's when they are most innovative. Slack also creates the space to discuss decisions and developments critically and calmly and to come up with refreshing and pioneering ideas and solutions. If the agenda is full, our heads are full too and there is insufficient space for reflection. If there is no room for a good conversation, then that's the first thing to open a conversation about.

27 Moral Muscle: The Importance of Sleep and Sugar

There's no shortage of good intentions: organizations want to satisfy customers, offer good working conditions, do honest business with suppliers, be environmentally responsible, contribute to society, and achieve good financial results. Organizations write these kinds of goals in their codes of conduct and take them as a starting point for their policy plans. But as with many other good intentions, such as giving up smoking, going on a diet, and being more sociable, it is easier said than done. The trick is to keep it up. Implementing good intentions in the long term is not just a matter of intention and motivation, but also of self-control and the discipline to resist emotions, habits, and impulses which frustrate one's attempts at achieving the goal. "I couldn't resist the temptation," "I gave way under pressure," and "I had a moment of weakness" are the statements of people whose self-control failed.

Tiredness is one of the reasons for the loss of self-control, resulting in increased chances of fraud and cheating. Nicole Mead and colleagues established this in their research. They began by making half of the participants in their study mentally tired. They did this by getting the participants to write a short essay without the letters A and N. Because these are common letters, the task required a great deal of energy. The other half had it easy; they too were required to write a short essay, but in their case without the rare letters X and Z. The participants were then required to complete the familiar math task (see Chapter 10) of finding the pairs which added up to 10 exactly within 5 minutes. For every question answered correctly the participants received 25 cents. Half of each group was required to hand in their answer forms so that the researchers could check them. The other half could check their own answers and pay themselves.

The non-tired participants in the self-checking group claimed to have completed 25 percent more correct tasks than the group checked by the researchers. Among the tired participants, however, the difference was much larger: those who were permitted to determine their own score claimed to have correctly completed no less than 104 percent more tasks than those judged by the researchers. The experiment shows that mental fatigue leads to reduced self-control. We become too tired to be honest. Our moral muscle deteriorates, causing us to succumb more readily to moments of weakness.

Experiments by Mark Muraven and Roy Baumeister show that self-control is sapped when it is tested frequently. The more we must control ourselves, the more strength it takes and the less remains for the following test, increasing the chance that we lose our self-control. In the end we can no longer find the strength to resist the temptation.

The good news is that we can train our self-control. Our moral muscles can increase in strength with exercise. By resisting small pressures and temptations, we build up strength in the form of self-confidence, experience, and resolve, so that we are subsequently able to resist greater pressures and temptations. Also by practicing with imaginary scenarios, for instance in dilemma training, our moral muscles are trained so that we are not so quick to cave in and can maintain our backbone.

Besides training, rest is important, as much for our moral as for our physical muscles. Research by William Killgore and colleagues shows that lack of sleep leads to slower moral decision making. In their study the participants were required to pass judgment on the behavior of others in a variety of difficult situations. Half of the group was well-rested, the other half had not been allowed to sleep for a long time. There was barely any difference in the time taken by the two groups to judge behavior in practical dilemmas, but in moral dilemmas the sleep-deprived participants took considerably longer to come to a judgment than those who were rested. Killgore's explanation is that tiredness makes it more difficult to integrate emotion and cognition, and it is this integration which is important in moral dilemmas.

People who regularly get too little sleep due to their work, and who are confronted with a variety of moral dilemmas, as are rescue workers, armed forces, and politicians, should therefore be extra alert to the risk of taking moral decisions more slowly and also differently from other people. The same goes for directors and managers who work long days and only get a short night's sleep. Even entire organizations can suffer fatigue, for instance from frequent reorganizations, and project and personnel changes. This fatigue comes at the cost of ethical decision making, as the decisions become too emotional and impulsive, or indeed too rational and detached.

Another thing that is important for our moral muscle is food. Research by Matthew Gailliot and Roy Baumeister shows that, like physical effort, activities which require self-control lower blood sugar levels. Discipline requires energy from our brains, which is supplied in the form of sugar. The lower the glucose level, the lower the self-control. A great deal of research shows that criminals, frauds, vandals, and traffic offenders, suffer more than average with hypoglycemia, low blood glucose. Sugar is therefore important for our self-control. When Gailliot and Baumeister gave the participants in their research a sugary drink, their blood sugar levels increased, and subsequently their self-control and moral behavior. This also explains the findings of another study, in which participants who skipped breakfast had less self-control. Not only is eating breakfast good, sugary food in the company canteen also helps to keep people on the straight and narrow (unless your goal is to lose weight).

Bertolt Brecht was therefore right. In his *Threepenny Opera* (Dreigroschenoper) the gangsters act like respectable businessmen and vice versa. The theme song is "Erst kommt das Fressen, dann kommt die Moral" (Food first, then morality). So it is important to establish that organizations do not suffer from hypoglycemia as well as a lack of sleep.

28 The Future Under Control: Implementation Plans and Coffee Cups

Organizations want and need to be increasingly under control. The goal for supervisors, directors, and managers is control over their organizations. All kinds of internal and external "in control statements" are issued, declaring that the organization is properly managed. But can an organization control behavior, not just now but in the future? What does it say if a company introduces a new code of conduct, a department resolves to implement an environmental program, or an employee declares that he will be more customer-oriented?

Besides the methods mentioned in the previous chapter, good resolutions stand or fall by their implementation plans. You may have thought they'd had their day. Don't those ritual rain dances just lead to bureaucracy and waste of time and energy? Aren't the new management styles "muddling through," "incremental management," and "entrepreneurial flexibility"? Research by Rob Holland and colleagues explains the psychology of implementation plans.

A telecoms company wanted to reduce its ecological footprint by making changes such as recycling more. They therefore decided to place a recycling bin for used plastic cups in each department. The bin was a short walk from each office worker's desk. Furthermore everyone was clearly and persuasively informed of the aim of this new bin; there was a special team set up to inform employees directly and instruct them in the importance and convenience of this bin. The company appeared to have taken reasonable measures to get the matter under control. But in spite of all efforts, no more was recycled than previously. Employees continued to throw their cups in the ordinary trash cans under their own desks. Even prominently placing a bin for plastic cups in each room did not help. The researchers wanted to help the company and thought of an approach which might work.

Some of the staff were asked to make a proposal as to when, where, and how they would recycle their plastic cups and to write this up. The researchers noted the effect of this on the behavior of the employees. At the end of each day they counted the plastic cups in the trash cans. Initially on average there were two plastic cups per day in each employee's own, general trash can, but after the researchers' intervention, this number decreased quickly. A week after the experiment began, the number of plastic cups was down to an eighth of the previous figure, while the number of cups was unchanged in the control group, where the old situation continued. In the second week the number of cups in the general trash can increased to an average of half a cup per person per day, but this average then remained constant, even two months later.

This experiment shows that if we wish to make our resolutions a reality we must translate these so-called "goal intentions" into "implementation intentions." This involves visualizing where, when, and how these goals will be achieved, and writing up a plan. Such implementation plans enable us to sustainably change behavior, even when it is behavior which asks more of us than walking to the recycle bin in the corridor to throw away a plastic cup. The strength of implementation plans is that we make our resolutions concrete. That means not only that the desired behavior is defined, but also that it is attached to the situation in which it will be exhibited ("In situation

X, I will do Y"). In this way we create a strong mental link between the situation and the desired behavior, so that when we get into that situation we also actually exhibit the desired behavior. If you want to change your behavior, you need to define both the desired behavior and the situations that require it. A person or organization which claims to behave honestly but cannot be more specific about this is making an empty gesture.

Implementation plans describe both what we will do and what we will no longer do. The latter point is not always obvious. In research by Bas Verplanken and Suzanne Faes, the participants made implementation plans for healthy eating. The positive result was that participants ate more healthy food. At the same time the participants did not eat less unhealthy food. The abstract goal (eat healthy) did not conflict with the concrete undesirable eating behavior (such as frequent snacking). We must also consciously leave behind our old behavior. Saying yes to one thing should mean saying no to another.

The power of making an implementation plan is in the commitment this creates. In the above experiment with the telecoms company, people agreed among themselves what they would do differently in the future. This in itself had an effect, although an agreement with yourself can be easy to ignore. But by making it concrete, you are reminded (especially initially) every time you consider violating the agreement with yourself. Throwing a cup into the general trash can then feel like a betrayal. If implementation plans are also publicly presented, commitment increases still further. Research shows that if people as a group proclaim that they will make a change, their chance of success increases. Violation of the agreement then not only feels like a betrayal of oneself, but also of the others.

Commitment also increases the more people are required to do to reach their goal. In their experiment Danny Axsom and Joel Cooper asked overweight women to participate in a new weight loss therapy. First they were asked to carry out a variety of unpleasant tasks, such as reading children's poetry out loud while the sound of their voice was played back to them with a short delay. The tasks produced irritation, stammering, and doubt. Half of the participants carried out this task for five sessions each lasting 1 hour. The other half also carried out this task over five sessions, but only for a few minutes each time. A year later all participants were weighed. The first group had lost a good 3 kilos, while the other group was only 150 grams lighter. The therapy had no connection with weight loss, but the participants who had been required to carry out the unpleasant tasks for longer, had to justify this to themselves, prompting them to make greater efforts to lose weight. The more effort and pain needed to arrive at a plan, the greater the chance that the plan will be realized. A plan that requires no personal sacrifice therefore often delivers little. Without a concrete *and* painful implementation plan, there is no sustainable or fundamental change in behavior. In short, successful resolutions benefit from a well thought through implementation plan. If you are judging the resolutions of others, ask the following questions: (a) Is there an implementation plan?, (b) In what situations will changes be made?, and (c) How much will it hurt?

29 Ethics on the Slide Leads to Slip-Ups: Escalating Commitment and the Induction Mechanism

"For a long time it was just small sums." These are the words of one of eight municipal collection clerks caught embezzling millions from the city parking meters. It began with taking the money that fell into the shaft of the parking meter when the moneybox was full and pocketing it for themselves. When the officials noticed how easy that was, they did it more often, until one of the officials wondered, "Why don't we take whole boxes?" Since the lock could be forced with a small pull, that was easy. The frequency with which the boxes were stolen soon increased. Despite the officials feeling that things were getting out of hand and that it would be better to stop, they continued, because "the extras were really rather nice." What began with pinching the overflow cash grew into a whole system for stealing the moneyboxes and sharing the spoils among the collection clerks. According to the municipality's calculations, the collection clerks were earning 8,000 euros per person per week before they were caught.

It is a common pattern: serious lapses begin with small slips. The greatest criminal starts out as a petty thief. Large-scale accounting fraud often begins with a trifling slip of the pen. Through practical research, Lawrence Sherman has defined six stages in the process of corruption of a police officer. It begins with (1) accepting small favors, such as free drinks and meals, followed by (2) intentionally ignoring shop closing times and illegal parking, (3) accepting money from driving offenders, (4) regularly accepting payment from casinos for tolerating abuses or even offering protection, (5) being bribed by prostitutes, brothel owners, and drug dealers, and finally (6) direct involvement in drug dealing.

There are at least two mechanisms which explain how people are sucked into such a downward spiral. The first mechanism is "escalating commitment": the feeling that there is no way back and one must go on. Once on the slide it is difficult to stop, let alone get back to the starting point. This was seen, for example, with stockbrokers (the rogue traders) who ran into trouble, such as Nick Leeson, Jérôme Kerviel, and Kweku Adoboli. Small losses are compensated for by taking greater risks, and if this leads to still greater losses, even greater risks are taken, and so it goes on. The example of Bernard Bradstreet, former head of a computer company, is well known.

According to friends, Bradstreet was an upstanding man with an untarnished reputation. Bradstreet wanted good figures to show when floating the company on the stock market. He therefore allowed his salespeople to book their sales ahead to a few days after the close of the quarter, without the other party signing for the sale. This meant that the profits came in slightly earlier, improving the quarterly figures. Because the other party had not yet signed, the products were transported to a warehouse where they would wait until the contract was completed. This action, however, led to the problem of reduced profits in the following quarter. After all, the salespeople started out behind. In order to be able to show equivalent quarterly figures, they now needed the sales of a few days into the next quarter plus a few extra. Days soon became weeks and months, and the fraud continued to grow. In the end the salespeople were so desperate that they were signing contracts on behalf of their customers.

The second mechanism that takes matters from bad to worse is the "induction mechanism." Escalating commitment means that there is no way back, even when one would like to turn things around. The induction mechanism changes the norms of those involved so that they no longer see their transgression as such. Under this mechanism, people use the behavior of the past as a point of comparison, as an anchor, for judging new behavior. If past behavior was ethical and acceptable, then equivalent or almost equivalent behavior is also ethical and responsible. If every step (away from what is ethical and acceptable) is small enough, then every new point reached is seen as ethical and can then serve as an acceptable starting point. If A is acceptable, and B somewhat less acceptable but still within reasonable bounds, then B is also acceptable. If C subsequently presents itself, perhaps somewhat less acceptable than B, but still within the bounds of possibility (as understood in relation to B), then C is fine, even if a single step from A to C would be unthinkable. A set of small steps can amount to a serious lapse. This can normalize corruption and erode standards without those involved recognizing it. Moral blindness is born.

Judson Mills has shown how this mechanism works on a small scale with the help of an experiment in an elementary school. Mills measured the attitude of the students to cheating. The students were then required to take an exam with prizes for the winners (a competitive set-up). Mills, however, had made the exam so difficult that it was almost impossible to win without cheating. The following day the students were asked again about their attitude to cheating. The students who had cheated now turned out to be more flexible in their attitude than previously. The students who had not cheated had not become more flexible. On the contrary, they were even more disapproving.

The above experiment shows that it is not only the case that values and norms influence our behavior: behavior also influences our values and norms. For this reason people can end up with very different values and norms from those they start out with. This means that we must be alert to small slips at work. Within organizations people are sometimes careless about small transgressions. But a small slip can be the first step on the way to a serious mistake in the future. Ethics on the slide leads to slip-ups. Because it is more and more difficult to stop on the slide, and impossible to go back, it is important to stay sharp and not allow oneself to become slack. As Leonardo da Vinci stated, "It is easier to resist at the beginning than at the end."

30 The Foot-in-the-Door and Door-in-the-Face Techniques: Self-Perception Theory

Salespeople often make use of the "lowball tactic": whether you are buying a new house, booking a vacation, or organizing a party, the salesperson first ensures that you make a choice before springing all kinds of supplementary additions on you which will cost you extra. You won't be able to fully enjoy your holiday without cancellation and travel insurance. Unfortunately the hotel you wanted is fully booked, but fortunately there is a hotel with rooms available in the neighborhood, even if it is somewhat more expensive. And when the booking is almost complete, all kinds of extra costs are added, such as tourist tax, travel agency costs, cleaning costs, a surcharge for the number of people, a high season surcharge, and so on. You didn't see that coming. But because you've shown a bit of enthusiasm, chances are you will bite in the end, in spite of the expense being more than you had planned for.

In the first exploratory experiment on this effect, carried out by Robbert Cialdini and colleagues in 1978, people were first asked to participate in a psychological experiment and after they agreed were asked to participate at seven o'clock in the morning because that was the only time slot available. This made them much more willing to agree to the request than people who were straightforwardly asked to take part in an experiment at seven o'clock in the morning. A commitment to the first request increases the chance that people will stick to it, even when the cost or sacrifice increases.

The lowball tactic is a way of getting people to do things they otherwise would not do, achieving "compliance without pressure," as it is known in the literature. Research by Jonathan Freedman and Scott Fraser illustrates another tactic to achieve the same results.

The researchers pretended to be volunteers for the neighborhood road traffic safety committee in an up-market residential area of California. They rang residents' doorbells and asked if they would take part in the campaign "Drive carefully in our neighborhood." This would require them to place signs in the neighborhood. And those signs must be big, so that drivers could not miss them. The volunteers then showed the residents a photo of a hideous sign of one by two meters, with the text "Drive carefully." The question was whether this sign could be placed in the resident's front garden. The sign might dominate the garden, but that was exactly what was needed to make drivers aware, according to the volunteers.

Initially 17 percent of the residents agreed to this request, but with a small change in approach the researchers succeeded in increasing this figure to 76 percent: a researcher had already been around a separate group of residents two weeks before, asking them whether they would be prepared to put a small poster in their window with the text "Be a safe driver." Because almost all residents agreed to cooperate with this, two weeks later three-quarters of this group agreed to place large signs in their gardens. The researchers here were making use of the so-called "foot-in-the-door technique."

The lowball tactic adds extra costs once a decision has been made. With the foot-in-the-door technique, the requests grow in scale, as do the costs. That's what happened in the previous experiment: agreeing to the small request changed the attitude of the residents. They began to see themselves as committed neighborhood residents and were therefore more motivated to contribute to the safety of their living environment. They also now had an image of themselves as people who agree to requests to contribute, so they tried to conform to this image in subsequent requests. People are strongly motivated to act in agreement with their self-image. This is explained by "self-perception theory": seeing yourself in a different way leads to behavior which enforces this new self-image. In the experiment self-perception was changed when people committed to a goal (increasing safety by a small sacrifice in the form of a poster in the window). The researchers could now make bigger requests, as long as they fitted into the residents' new self-image.

The foot-in-the-door tactic can be used to nudge people toward better behavior, but also to get people to commit increasingly big transgressions. If someone is asked to commit a small misdemeanor out of loyalty to his boss, for example, his self-perception changes. This might conjure up a self-image of someone exceptionally loyal, unafraid of getting his hands dirty. That in turn opens the way to larger requests which further emphasize and strengthen this image. In such situations people have the feeling that they can demonstrate their loyalty by doing things which others would refuse.

Stanley Milgram's experiment, described in Chapter 18, also used this foot-in-the-door tactic: the participants were not asked to administer a shock of 450 volts the first time, because in that case the majority would probably have dropped out immediately. By requesting gradual increases, it became more and more difficult for the participants to draw the line. Why would you not administer a shock of 330 volts if you had just administered one of 300 volts?

There is a third tactic which can be effective: the door-in-the-face tactic. Here an enormous request is made first, which will certainly be refused. However, this makes people more inclined to accept a smaller request, which they would not otherwise have consented to. Robert Cialdini and colleagues researched this. They found that students who refused the request to do two years of volunteer work as a lawyer for young offenders were considerably more willing to supervise a group of young offenders for a 2-hour visit to the zoo than students who were only approached with the latter request.

The door-in-the-face tactic is effective because the first request gets people to engage in self-reflection ("Do I want to do volunteer work, do I think this is important, what am I prepared to contribute?"). Even if they refuse to go to the great effort of contributing two years, the request activates their self-image as someone who is prepared to do volunteer work, as long as the time commitment remains within reasonable bounds. The second, smaller request fits precisely with that new picture and for that reason they grasp it with both hands. Moreover their initial refusal arouses a feeling of guilt. The second request offers an opportunity to compensate.

The three tactics can be applied in many respects in work: for example there are organizations which present a very ambitious code of conduct in one go (the door-in-the-face tactic). Even if not everything in it can be achieved, it encourages people to do their very best, leading to better results than if they were following a more modest code. Other organizations start with a conservative code of conduct, with the idea that the bar can be raised once support has been won and the code followed. By periodically adjusting the code, everyone keeps pace with it, preventing the organization overreaching itself. By deploying the lowball tactic the organization first allows the employees to declare that they will follow the code. It subsequently becomes apparent that bigger sacrifices are necessary for compliance than was originally thought. Because the employees have now committed themselves, they are more willing to make the increasing investments, thereby further increasing their commitment.

By asking the right questions we can get people to do things which they otherwise would not do. However, we must take care not to trap our feet or bang our heads, with all the opening and closing doors.

31 So Long as the Music Is Playing: Sound Waves and Magnetic Waves

"So long as the music is playing, you've got to get up and dance." This was the reply of the CEO of the biggest bank in the world in July 2007 to a question over problems in the mortgage market and financing private equity deals. According to Larry Elliott and Dan Atkinson, authors of *The Gods that failed: How blind faith in markets has cost us our future*, the "music" of liquidity seduced the financial sector. This led to blind faith, and all the risks that come with it.

The CEO was in some sense right: before liquidity dried up in 2008, it was very difficult to work against the market. Shareholders and investors had no patience with those planning for the possibility of stagnation in the economy and taking fewer risks than their colleagues. As far as they were concerned, careful traders should clear out. The well-known economist John Maynard Keynes (1883–1946) warned that the market can be irrational for longer than people are solvent. As long as there is music, people must move to it. "We're still dancing," the CEO added to his previous statement. Not long after his remark, the music stopped and the CEO was asked to leave the dance floor.

Lack of room for maneuver is often used as an excuse for failure to change. "We'd like to invest in the environment, but the market doesn't allow it," "We'd like to do business more respectably, but the market doesn't allow it," and "We'd like to deliver better quality to our customers, but the market ..." It is often doubtful whether change is really impossible or whether this is just what people want to hear. Even if you can't make *the* difference, you can still make *a* difference.

The danger of the metaphor of dancing to the music is that the music is seen as a fact in itself, casting the organization and its employees into the role of mere listeners. Critics rightly point to the importance of the tone at the top, since it is the top of the organization that determines the tone of the music and thus the atmosphere in the work environment. But does music only have a metaphorical meaning, or can it literally determine people's behavior? Charles Areni and David Kim wanted to find out, and decided to research the relationship between music and consumer behavior.

In their experiment they varied the background music in a wine shop. For half the visitors they played classical music, and for the other half pop music. The researchers pretended to be shop assistants busy making an inventory of the stock. In reality they observed the visitors and registered the number of bottles taken from the shelves, which labels were read, and how long the customers stayed in the shop. The background music turned out to have no influence on any of these factors. It did not even influence the number of bottles bought. However, the researchers discovered another effect: the music turned out to affect the price of wine bought. When classical music was played, people bought wine on average three times the price of that bought when pop music was playing. According to the researchers, classical music leads customers to believe subconsciously that they have more refined, distinguished tastes, in turn prompting them to purchase more expensive wine, which better fits their self-image.

Background music therefore determines people's self-image and consequently their behavior. Organizations can use this to influence people's behavior to their advantage, by choosing the right music in lifts, toilets, the canteen, shop, waiting room, factory floor, or reception. Music can be a way of steering people's behavior, as they wait on the phone or visit a website. There are even directors who have music playing in their offices all day long. If you too have music playing at work, please be aware that too much country music is inadvisable. Research by Steven Stack and Jim Gundlach shows that listening to depressing country music lyrics played a role in half of suicides in the United States.

Besides sound waves, magnetic waves can also affect our morals. Liane Young and colleagues researched this subject. They stimulated the part of the brain known as the "right temporoparietal junction" in their participants using a magnetic field. While they did this, the participants were required to listen to stories and judge whether the main character had good or bad intentions. The participants exposed to the magnetic waves had difficulty recognizing malicious intentions if the intentions had no consequences. For example, the main character in one story tried to kill her friend with a white powder which she thought was poisonous. In the end it turned out to be icing sugar. Because her friend did not become sick, most participants exposed to magnetic waves thought that the woman's action was morally acceptable, whereas the participants who were not exposed to the magnetic field tended to reject this action as morally wrong.

According to the researchers, their results show that people's morality can be manipulated by disturbing brain activity. They point out, however, that we need not fear that our consciences are being manipulated: the technique they used cannot be applied secretly. Organizations who would like to positively influence the consciences of their employees and visitors must therefore be patient. For now they will have to do it with music.

Factor 4: Commitment

In the previous section we saw how important it is that people in organizations have the means and opportunities to carry out their duties successfully and responsibly. Sufficient time must be allowed, and the type of goal is important. One-sided goals and those that are set too high increase the chance of improper behavior. It is essential that people are prevented from embarking on a slippery slope and landing up in trouble, unable to climb back up.

Desirable behavior in an organization not only depends on the extent to which people know what is expected (clarity and role-modeling) and are able to adhere to it (achievability), but also on the extent to which they are *motivated* to fulfill expectations. This brings us to the fourth factor which affects behavior in organizations: commitment. Commitment is the motivation to invest effort in the interests of the organization. The more respectfully an organization treats its employees, the more it involves them in decision making and the more it offers in terms of positive identification with the company, the more effort employees will invest.

The following six chapters present experiments illustrating the significance of commitment. Chapter 32 is devoted to the importance of a good mood and atmosphere in the workplace. Chapter 33 shows how important it is that people can identify with the organization. We learn that the organization must have a face for this to work. Chapter 34 explains how personal contact and personal attention can lead to greater commitment from employees. Chapter 35 shows how commitment can be achieved with an unusual technique, using scents. In Chapter 36 we see that commitment is undermined when employees have a sense of injustice within the organization. Finally, Chapter 37 explains how people who see themselves as committed and honest can still behave improperly.

32 Feeling Good and Doing Good: Mood and Atmosphere

Plenty of research points to the effects of workplace atmosphere on creativity, flexibility, and commitment among employees. People in a good mood estimate the chance of positive developments higher than people in a bad mood, and the chance of negative developments lower. The thinking is that people in a good mood behave more sociably and morally than people in a bad mood. People in a bad mood are more wrapped up in themselves and more inclined to behave immorally and antisocially in order to cheer themselves up. But does a good mood really lead to more sociable and moral behavior? Research into tipping in restaurants hints at a possible answer.

You might expect restaurant tips to depend on the quality of food and service, but various studies show that the customer's mood is also important. Nicolas Guéguen, for example, carried out research in a French bar. The staff were asked to give the client a card with the check. Some of the cards displayed an advertisement for a local nightclub, and others the following joke: "An Eskimo had been waiting for his girlfriend in front of a movie theater for a long time, and it was getting colder and colder. After a while, shivering with cold and rather infuriated, he opened his coat and drew out a thermometer. He then said loudly, 'If she is not here at 15, I'm going'!" Guéguen noted the reactions of customers and the amount they gave as a tip. Customers who received the joke on average gave 50 percent more than customers who received the nightclub advertisement. Furthermore, when the joke was given the number of customers who tipped rose from 25 percent to 42 percent, whereas among customers who had received the nightclub card this fell to 19 percent. Happy eaters are clearly more generous givers.

Another study by Guéguen, this time in collaboration with Patrick Legoherel, shows that service with a smile or the word "Thank you" on the check also encouraged higher tips. The tip rises significantly, by almost 60 percent, if the waiter introduces himself. The weather also affects mood and people's tipping behavior: when the sun shines, or even when the waiter just says the sun is shining or is going to shine, the tip increases.

The principle of "feeling good and doing good" is also illustrated by Alice Isen and Paula Levin. Subjects who found money in a telephone booth were more willing to help someone they saw dropping things in the street. The difference was quite significant: only 4 percent of subjects who had not found money helped, compared to 84 percent of those who had. This research has been repeated many times with approximately the same results.

Three explanations are offered as to why good feelings generate good deeds. First, when we feel good, we are more optimistic and have a higher opinion of other people, making us more willing to do something nice for them. Second, when we feel good, we want to hold onto the feeling, and this can be achieved by doing a good deed. Third, when we feel good, we spend more time on ourselves and are more aware of our values and norms. Because doing good is an important value for many people, a greater awareness of this leads people to do more good. Extending this idea to the workplace, the better employees feel, the more they will be inclined to do good deeds for others. For this reason good working conditions are important for realizing an organization's financial and social goals, and the interests and expectations of external stakeholders are also better served in a good atmosphere.

However, there are potential risks, as shown by Georgina Craciun in her research into the flipside of a good mood. In her experiment, participants were required to do an IQ test, check their own answers and report the results to the researchers. Participants were permitted to throw their answers in the trash can and pass their score to the researchers on a separate sheet of paper, but the researchers were able to see which answer forms belonged together by a perforation on both sheets. Before the test the participants were given about 10 minutes to write a story. One group was asked to write about a positive event, and the other about a negative event. The prediction was that the mood this created would influence the participants' behavior. And indeed, of the participants in a bad mood, 13 percent cheated on their test results, as compared to 36 percent of those in a good mood.

According to Craciun, people in a positive mood think of themselves more positively than people in a negative mood. They walk around with their head in the clouds believing there will be no end to it. People in a positive mood also reflect less on the negative consequences of their actions. And when they do reflect, they estimate the chance of being caught lower than those in a negative mood. So in an organization with a positive atmosphere, the management or regulator is best advised to draw extra attention to the negative consequences of misdemeanors and the measures taken to catch offenders.

33 A Personal Face: Social Bond Theory and Lost Property

Research shows that many employees would not recognize the chief of their organization if they passed him in the street. What does it say if the boss, or even the organization, has no face? Experiments by Richard Wiseman give us an indication of the answer.

Wiseman and his team left wallets in the streets of the Scottish city of Edinburgh to see whether these would be returned by the finders. There was no money inside, but the wallets did contain other valuables such as discount vouchers, lottery tickets, and cards. What Wiseman wanted to know is whether wallets which were easy to link to a person were returned more often. He investigated this by placing a photo in some of the wallets.

The results were surprising: only 15 percent of the wallets without photos were returned. Wallets containing evidence of a donation to a good cause were returned slightly more frequently (20 percent), and wallets with a photo of an elderly person somewhat more frequently, at 28 percent. The wallets with a family photo did considerably better: 48 percent of these were returned. But the real cracker was yet to come: a wallet with a photo of a young child produced returns at 88 percent.

What do these results tell us? The bad news is that wallets without photos are almost never returned. The good news is that a wallet with a photo of a baby is almost always returned. The explanation offered is that the photo inspires caring feelings, appealing to the finder's sense of responsibility.

The research therefore shows people are more inclined to help someone with whom they can identify. The converse is also true: the more anonymous and distant a relationship, the less the sense of responsibility. As Mother Teresa said, "If I look at the mass I will never act. If I look at the one, I will."

In larger organizations this can really be a problem. Employees and customers feel more like a number than an individual. As a result of upscaling, mergers, and expansions, departments and units grow, making employees feel lost in the crowd. And with the trumpeted new modes of working, with flexible office hours and workstations, employees may end up feeling lost and left behind.

According to "social bond theory," developed by Travis Hirschi, people behave antisocially within a community when they do not feel a bond with it. If people feel detached from the community, literally or figuratively homeless, they will break the rules more easily, or form bonds with groups that hold norms and values destructive to society (such as gangs and other criminal organizations). People adopt the norms and values of those they feel connected with. The more employees feel a bond with their organization, the more they will commit to the goals of their employer. All kinds of undesirable behavior, such as theft, fraud, and neglect of duty, can spring from the lack of a bond with the organization.

In order to make solidarity, commitment, and responsibility possible, it is therefore necessary to allow people to identify with the organization. One way of achieving this is by giving the organization a face, an identity, a recognizable profile, by showing some personal color, and making personal contact with employees and external stakeholders. An insurance company successfully achieved this: customers no longer need to send in receipts or fill in forms, they can simply report the damage over the phone. This personal contact reduces fraud and gives the organization a voice and a face for customers, making it harder to lie.

Another example is the effect of the daily weblogs or tweets some managers write. Their power lies in the fact that these are not texts written by communication experts, combed through and smoothed out by lawyers or anyone else wishing to contribute to the decision as to what is communicated. Authentic messages give an insight into the world of the people involved and a face to the organization.

This is also true for the supporting departments in an organization: if they lack a face, employees take their instructions less seriously; in fact, they will be less inclined to approach the department at all. Sometimes it is easy to bridge the gap by sending supporting department employees out into the organization, having them introduce themselves, and getting them to give presentations about their department and ask about the expectations and views of their department. This quickly raises the department's profile.

In short, the question is not only what photos someone has in his wallet, but more importantly, whether or not an organization has a face in its dealings with employees and external stakeholders.

34 Cows and Post-It Notes: Love in the Workplace

There is a Dutch saying, "You milk a cow through her mouth." The meaning is simple: the more you feed them and the higher the quality of the food, the more milk will be produced and the higher its quality. Plain as day. Isn't it? Well no, that's not the only thing that determines the milk yield, as shown in research by Catherine Bertenshaw and Peter Rowlinson. They carried out research among more than 500 farmers in England. What did they discover? Farmers who name their cows have a higher milk yield than famers with unnamed cows. The difference is significant: 280 liters per year. Addressing people by name also works; it increases satisfaction and loyalty. So if you want more satisfied customers, address them personally. The same goes for more satisfied and harder working employees.

Is it really that simple? Apparently not, and perhaps that's not such a bad thing. Returning to cows, addressing the cow by name is not really the cause of the higher milk production, but rather a consequence of the way in which the farmer treats his cattle. The researchers discovered that cows produced more milk when the farmer emphasized their individuality, gave them personal attention, stroked them and cared for them. This improved the well-being of the cow and her view of people. The cow became happier and more relaxed, improving her milk production. Farmers who name their cows do so in order to express the care and love they have for their animals, but it does not follow that a name necessarily generates care and love. Any farmer who thinks his milk production can be increased just by going round naming his cows can forget it. This does not change his level of care and attention for them.

People's happiness and well-being, be they customers, patients, colleagues, or students, cannot simply be increased by addressing them by name. It is a matter of the love and care they receive. Take note: if someone shows love and care for the sake of increasing the commitment and performance of another, that is not genuine love. Love comes from the heart. The behavior is counterproductive if it is seen as disingenuous. That's why servant leadership is almost impossible to teach. Either you get it or you don't.

Still, a bit of personal attention can work wonders. This is shown by Joyce Croonen and Liza Luesink in their research for a national tax authority. Normally taxpayers receive a letter annually requesting a tax return before a given date. Many tax returns, however, are not returned on time. Could this problem be solved with a personal note? The researchers decided to place a Post-it note on the standard letter, with a handwritten request to file the tax return on time. This doubled the speed of filings. Personal attention appears to work, and can be achieved with the smallest of gestures, such as dropping by a colleague's office to catch up.

We return once more to the cows. Bertenshaw and Rowlinson's study showed that two-thirds of the participating farmers formed warm personal bonds with all their livestock. As one farmer interviewed said, "The animals aren't just cattle to us, they're part of the family." If we look at the hardening of society, the level of customer friendliness, and the bleak work climate in many organizations, it seems that they could learn a lesson from these farmers.

35 The Place Stinks: Smell and Association

Smells affect consumer behavior. Research shows that people order more if the restaurant smells of lavender, the smell of freshly baked bread in the supermarket promotes sales and the scent of pineapple spread via the air conditioning in prisons makes the prisoners happier, more positive and less nervous. Smells also affect work performance. It has been shown that employees in administrative functions make up to 21 percent fewer typing errors in the presence of lemon scent. For this reason more and more companies are adopting a "house scent" (a corporate identity scent), which is spread by special devices in the workplace. There are even consultancies for business scents.

If smells affect our behavior, do they also affect our ethics and our moral behavior? Katie Liljenquist and colleagues researched this issue and came up with the following experiment.

Participants were placed in a room and received money from an unknown person from the room next door. All participants were told that this unknown person had received 4 dollars from those running the experiment and had decided to send them the full amount. This amount was tripled by those running the experiment. The participants were required to decide how much money to return to the anonymous person and what to keep for themselves. So participants could exploit the unknown person by keeping all the money or they could honor the trust placed in them by returning some portion. When the subjects were placed in a stuffy room, they gave back 2.81 dollars on average. In a fresh-smelling room, where the researchers had sprayed lemon scent, the average sum returned was 5.33 dollars. Almost double!

In a second experiment the subjects were given the opportunity to donate to a good cause. Again the subjects in the fresh-smelling room gave higher sums than those in the stuffy room, although on inquiry it appeared that the subjects had not been aware of the scent.

Smell also apparently affects the way we make judgments. In a study by Wen Li and colleagues, subjects were presented with various photos of people, and required to indicate how likeable they found them. In rooms with a lemon scent people were judged to be more likeable than in rooms with the odor of sweat. Another study shows that women who smell of herbs are estimated to be five years younger. People also judge the behavior of others less harshly if they are in a fresh-smelling environment.

How does smell affect our behavior? Scents activate our memory. These associations are almost unbreakable: the smell of chalk puts people in mind of their primary school days, the smell of baby oil conjures up images of early parenthood, and the scent of an item of clothing belonging to a loved one who has died stirs up all kinds of emotions. We also associate certain scents, such as those of lemon and lime, with cleanliness, freshness, and purity. The parts of the brain which recognize the scent are activated at the same time as the parts of the brain which affect behavior. Because we are used to smelling lemon when cleaning, just the smell is enough to get us rolling our sleeves up. Accustomization to the combination means the smell alone activates the associated behavior. Such associations can even be extended so that physical cleanliness, for example, comes to be associated with moral cleanliness: a fresh environment leads to more sociable behavior and milder judgments.

A fresh workplace encourages fresh behavior. In order to encourage ethical and sociable behavior, it is therefore important to create a pleasant-smelling environment. Perhaps it is even an idea to stipulate a lemon scent in the code of conduct. The important thing, of course, is to regularly open the windows and give the meeting rooms and other places where important decisions are taken a good airing. Don't let it get too cold though: people are milder and friendlier toward one another in a warm room than in a cold one. Physical cold is associated with cold behavior, so people tend to be less friendly.

So on your wanderings pay attention to your nose, as well as your eyes and ears. Does it smell fresh or stuffy? Smell affects behavior, and behavior also affects the scent of the room. There's a reason why we say that a business "stinks," or something smells "fishy," when dubious practices have taken place. The odor of sweat is suspicious, as people sweat when they have committed a misdemeanor. And smelling a rat will do no good either.

36 Wealth is Damaging: Red Rags and Red Flags

There are plenty of imposing office buildings: spacious, with high ceilings, and luxurious down to the last detail, each company competing to dominate the skyline. This is a way for an organization to gain exposure, demonstrating its presence and achieving recognition. A beautiful building is a pleasure to work in and impresses visitors. It declares the organization's identity and ambitions.

But does every organization achieve what it wants with this? That depends partly on how employees interpret the office building and their working environment. Francesca Gino and Lamar Pierce wanted to know if an extravagantly luxurious working environment led to unethical behavior. They therefore set up the following experiment.

Participants were required to make as many anagrams as possible in eight rounds of 2 minutes. They had seven letters from which to make as many words as possible, using each letter only once in each word. Each time the participants came up with 12 words, they received 3 dollars. After 8 rounds, the participants were given 20 minutes to check their work with a dictionary, and were then permitted to pay themselves.

The participants were required to write down the number of correct answers on an answer form, to preserve anonymity, and give this to the researchers afterwards. They were also required to deposit their notes with the words they thought up in a sealed box at the front of the room. Because every participant received a unique set of letters in the final round, the researchers were able to match up the papers with the answer forms.

So far, a standard experiment. What was unusual about this experiment was what the participants saw on entering the room. A researcher stood waiting at the entrance, by a table with money on it. For each participant who entered, he picked up 24 one-dollar bills. This was the maximum amount that each participant could earn. In the so-called "poor" situation, once each participant had received their pile of bills and everyone had sat down, all the money on the researcher's table had been used up. The other participants, entering the "wealthy" situation, saw the researcher take the 24 dollar bills from an enormous pile of 7,000 bills. The question was which situation would see the most cheating.

In the poor situation the participants on average exaggerated their score by 14 percent. In the wealthy situation this was more than double, at 31 percent. Over all the rounds in the poor situation 39 percent of the participants exaggerated at least once, while in the wealthy situation the figure was 85 percent. An affluent, luxurious situation apparently creates twice as many cheats. It was noteworthy that both groups exaggerated their scores in three rounds on average: it was the *magnitude* of the exaggeration, not the number of instances of cheating, that made the difference. In the poor situation 26 percent of the participants exaggerated their score for at least four answers, while in the wealthy situation the figure was 80 percent.

The results of this study offer an explanation as to why organizations with an air of luxury and wealth inspire employees to behave unethically. This applies not only to the place of work, but also to rewards, perks, and investments. Excess can lead to feelings of injustice, when employees have the feeling that they are not benefiting from the wealth. These feelings of injustice can lead to jealousy, indignation, inferiority, and envy, which pave the way to unethical behavior. Unethical behavior highlights the emotional stress such feelings inspire. This behavior can consist of hostility, sabotage, neglect, fraud, and theft. In the experiment the behavior of the researchers, who handled the large amount of money they appeared to possess quite casually, led to jealousy among the participants, who had to work hard for it.

Another possible explanation for the fact that wealth leads to unethical behavior comes from research by Kathleen Vohs. In her experiments she showed that the mere image of money leads to more selfish behavior. Money makes people think of success (because money is often the reward for success) and individual needs (because money is a means of satisfying one's needs). The more money, the greater the chance that people will be selfish. People may also rationalize the seriousness of their misdemeanor with the argument that the disadvantaged party has so much that the damage of helping oneself to a piece of the pie is relatively small.

It is important that people at the top of an organization are aware of the risks of conspicuous spending. They must understand that this sets particular psychological mechanisms in motion among employees, suppliers and customers. It can even attract criminality. Wealth and luxury can work as a red rag to a bull, and that's why they are red flags.

37 Morals on Vacation: Cognitive Dissonance and Rationalizations

How can a CFO siphon off money year after year into a private account without anyone once doubting his integrity? How can a scientist falsify his data for years, publishing it in top journals, without anyone once doubting his integrity? How can an investor pockets clients' money instead of investing it for more than 25 years without anyone once doubting his integrity?

The theory of "cognitive dissonance" helps us to explain such behavior. Cognitive dissonance refers to the discomfort arising from holding conflicting cognitions. Cognitions are pieces of knowledge, ideas, or convictions. Cognitive dissonance arises under a conflict between beliefs, or between belief and behavior (believing one thing and doing another). These contradictory cognitions force our minds to seek out new thoughts or ideas, or to adjust our current beliefs to reduce the dissonance between the cognitions. For example, if we want to stop smoking (cognition) but are unable to resist the temptation to light up again (behavior), this causes tension between cognition and behavior. If we want to engage in honest business practices (cognition) but still decide to take the competition for a ride (behavior), there is a conflict which we must reduce or remove, because we cannot cope with the feeling of unease it causes. Cognitive dissonance irritates, causes stress and saps energy. It can even harm people's positive self-image. We find it difficult to live with ourselves when we consider ourselves worthless. We want to see ourselves as rational and honest, so we think up reasons, often subconsciously, to reconcile the conflicting cognitions.

Research shows that chain smokers who tried to stop smoking failed because they managed to play down the risks of smoking to themselves. We call this "rationalization": we come up with a reason for unreasonable behavior. We talk black into white and vice versa. A great deal of research has been done on the rationalization and neutralization techniques people apply. Classic research among young offenders by Gresham Sykes and David Matza from the 1950s illustrates five rationalizations. Denying one's own responsibility ("It's not my fault"); denying the damage or disadvantage to the other party ("No one will suffer for this," "What they don't know won't hurt them"); denying a victim ("They asked for it," "You get what you deserve"); condemning those who condemn the misdemeanor ("They should take a look at themselves," "He started it"); and blaming their action on loyalty to another ("I didn't do it for myself"). Later research among other groups brought a number of other rationalizations to light. Often the image of a balance is raised ("On balance I've done more good than bad"); people point to others ("Everyone does it"); negative intentions are denied ("It was only a joke"); and people call on relative acceptability ("Others are worse than me"). If this kind of argument is used in the workplace, then it's time to intervene to address the flimsiness of the arguments and ideas.

Leon Festinger was the founder of cognitive dissonance theory. A classic experiment by Festinger and Merrill Carlsmith shows how quickly rationalizations occur and how quickly they lead to adjusted norms when people are unable to find external justifications. The participants were required to continually turn a number of pegs 90 degrees for 20 minutes. This was a pointless and boring exercise. The participants were subsequently asked to convince a new participant that this exercise was very interesting, to get this person to set to work too. Half the participants were given the prospect of earning 1 dollar for this, and the other half 20 dollars. Afterwards the participants were asked how interesting they actually found turning the pegs. What were the results? The participants who received 20 dollars found the exercise less interesting than the participants who received 1 dollar. This is surprising. Surely the participants all did the same exercise? What happened? The participants who received 20 dollars could justify lying to the other person by the high sum they received for it. The other group had no external reason strong enough to lie, so they had to convince themselves. They achieved this by telling themselves that turning the pegs was actually quite fun. This made them believe they were telling the truth to the newcomers.

Festinger and Carlsmith's experiment shows the danger of rationalizations. We can lie with dry eyes because we have made ourselves blind to the truth. We take a moral day off, as Sykes and Matza call it. Moral objections are swept under the table or temporarily switched off. The greater the cognitive dissonance, the greater the motivation to close this gap. People use rationalizations to build up protection against accusations, from themselves and others. This promotes moral blindness and opens the door to new transgressions. Morals are sent on vacation, and we continue to see ourselves as honest. As Bernard Ebbers said to his fellow church-goers, after the fraud at his company became known, "I just want you to know you aren't going to church with a crook. No one will find me to have knowingly committed fraud." In the end he was convicted of fraud and sentenced to 25 years in prison.

Rationalizations can embed themselves deep in the fabric of an organization, making them seem perfectly normal. The problem with rationalizations is that they soothe our consciences to sleep. When someone says that his behavior does not keep him awake at night, that does not necessarily say anything about his behavior. In order to break through rationalizations it is important to be aware of their existence and the underlying conflicting cognitions. One way of achieving this is to reveal hypocrisy. Chris Dickerson and colleagues demonstrate this in a simple experiment.

The enormous water usage at a campus sports complex was a big problem. Signs were placed all round the building instructing students to use water responsibly. The effect was very limited. Only 15 percent of the students shortened their shower time. The researchers therefore decided to apply two different methods. Students in the first group were stopped on the way to the shower and asked to sign a petition against wasting water. This activated awareness of the norm. A second group of students was asked to fill out a questionnaire on water usage. This raised their awareness of their own behavior. Both methods were immediately effective. Instead of showering for 5.01 minutes, students now showered for 4.08 minutes. But what happened when both methods were applied at the same time? Water usage dropped still further, to 3.40 minutes. This tapped the students' sense of hypocrisy by emphasizing the gap between their own behavior and the norm.

So when it forms the motivation to bring behavior in line with the desired norms, a sense of hypocrisy can be a positive thing, although we must take care that the dissonance is not resolved in the wrong direction. Hypocrisy can also form the motivation to water down the norm and to bring it more into line with current behavior. What should we make of the following statement made by a politician: "My principles are so high that I can always squeeze under them if I need to?"

Factor 5: Transparency

The previous section addressed the factor of "commitment." We saw that it is important that employees feel committed to the organization. This can be achieved by, for example, servant leadership, personal contact and attention, respectful treatment, introducing the right scents in the workplace and giving the organization a personal face.

Even when an organization has achieved clarity, role modeling, achievability, and commitment, undesirable behavior can still rear its head. It is important that this is noticed. This brings us to the fifth factor: transparency. Transparency is the extent to which people are able to see the effects of their own behavior as well as the behavior of others. Transparency is important because it makes adjustment and correction possible, and because it increases people's awareness and sense of responsibility.

In the following five chapters, several experiments are discussed which illustrate the meaning of transparency. Chapter 38 discusses why it is imperative that people look themselves in the eye. Chapter 39 is about looking one another in the eye and the corrective effect this has. Chapter 40 shows how people weigh up the chance of getting caught when they decide to do wrong. Chapter 41 adds a critical note to the significance of transparency. Finally in Chapter 42 a few perverse effects of transparency are presented.

38 The Mirror as a Reality Check: Objective Self-Awareness and Self-Evaluation

One organization has something rather original on the final page of its code of conduct: a mirror. Whatever employees decide, they must always be able to look themselves in the eyes. Does this work? Do mirrors foster better behavior or do they increase laziness and complacency? For the answer we turn to an experiment by Arthur Beaman and colleagues, carried out at Halloween.

As people all over the United States were decorating their houses with creepy objects such as spiders and witches, and children were preparing to go knocking on doors in the hope of receiving candy, Beaman and colleagues decorated the gardens of 18 houses. When children called at these houses, the research assistant opened the door and asked the children their names. She pointed to a big bowl of candy and told the children they could take one piece each. She then said that she had to get back to work and closed the door. The children were now alone and could help themselves to more candy unobserved. Or so they thought. The researchers watched them through a peephole.

What did they discover? A third of the children took more than one piece of candy. Nothing groundbreaking so far. Beaman and colleagues were interested in whether they could reduce the number of thieving children. At a number of houses they placed a mirror by the bowl of candy. When taking candy the children could not avoid seeing themselves in the mirror. Would this reduce the number of stealing children? This indeed turned out to be the case. Now only 9 percent took more than one piece of candy.

The placement of a simple object led to a significant reduction in stealing because the mirror encouraged self-awareness and self-evaluation. "Self-awareness theory" states that when we direct our attention to ourselves, we judge our current behavior and compare it against our internal values and norms. We become aware of the gap between who we want to be and what we are actually doing. This awareness begins to develop from around the age of 18 months. At this stage children no longer see another person when they look in the mirror, but begin to understand that they are looking at themselves. That's why psychologists call this development the "mirror stage." People can reduce their self-awareness through distractions such as watching TV, playing video games, or using alcohol and drugs. Seeing oneself in mirrors, watching oneself on video or hearing tapes of oneself raises self-awareness (which is why people sometimes find it confrontational). The resulting self-evaluation increases the chance that people feel motivated to live up to their own values and norms. So it can't do any harm to look yourself in the eyes for a minute or so after a day's work and ask yourself if you really stand by everything you did that day. Better still, you could look yourself in the eyes first thing in the morning, to remind yourself of what you stand for that day.

The use of mirrors is especially effective at the moment that decisions are made, when people are tempted, and when they are under pressure. So there's no harm in placing mirrors in the toilets, but it might be an idea to place them in the meeting room, the directors' rooms, the shop floor, and the warehouse too.

Besides hanging up mirrors, reflection is also effective in a figurative sense: self-evaluation, introspection, examining, and scrutinizing oneself and one another can be very fruitful. Reflection improves self-awareness and commitment to the desired norms (even if rationalizations still lie in wait). It is important to reflect on what is and is not done in the long term as well as the short term. Research shows that when people judge their behavior over the short term, they feel more sorry about things they have done (and should not have) than about the things they omitted to do (but should have). In the long term, however, this is reversed.

For many organizations the challenge is to create space for self-reflection. This can easily be forgotten in the heat of the moment. Personal plans for the year disappear under time pressure and project evaluations do not take place because the following project should already have begun. Full agendas prevent a moment of contemplation. It is not always easy to hold a mirror up to oneself or another. It can be confrontational. It is therefore necessary to find the time and the courage before it's too late.

39 Constrained by the Eyes of Strangers: The Four Eyes Principle

Looking someone in the eye is a powerful persuasive technique. Research shows, for example, that motorists are more likely to stop for a hitchhiker who looks them in the eye than one who looks away. Eye contact appears to make pedestrians more likely to take a brochure and allow people asking for money to collect more cash more easily. In short, if you want to ask someone a favor, eye contact is more effective than an email or phone conversation. But does eye contact promote moral behavior? Melissa Bateson and colleagues carried out the following experiment to investigate this.

The employees of a psychology faculty were required to place money in a pot when they made a cup of coffee or tea. However, the takings were slim. This had to do with the rather remote position of the common room, which allowed employees to ignore the rules unseen. The researchers wanted to know if they could improve payment behavior by applying a simple intervention. First they hung a large poster with a picture of flowers at eye level above the money pot. Every two weeks they replaced the poster with a different floral print. Payment behavior remained unchanged. Then the researchers changed tack: every other week they hung a different poster with a photo of a pair of eyes. On one occasion they were a man's eyes, another time a woman's. On one occasion the person appeared friendly, another time rather tense. In all cases the eyes looked directly into the lens.

What did the results show? The sum in the money pot rose, by no less than 275 percent.

According to the researchers an image of eyes gives people the feeling that they are not alone, and that their behavior is being observed. Another study shows that even the idea of someone watching has this effect. Research among three-year-old children shows that when they were told that there was an invisible princess in the room, they were less inclined to behave secretively. Students told that the ghost of a dead student had been observed in the examination room cheated less in their exam than students who were not told this. Study participants required to write sentences which made them think of God subsequently behaved far more altruistically than when they had not done this (regardless of whether or not they were religious).

The eyes of another work as a mechanism for moral guidance, arousing feelings of social control, and with them guilt and shame for irresponsible behavior.

Looking another person deep in the eyes has the effect of increasing a person's honesty and integrity. So in addition to hanging mirrors in the places where important decisions are made, as suggested in the previous chapter, a few photos of the eyes or even faces of stakeholders might not go amiss. The converse also applies: people who avoid eye contact often have something on their conscience. It is therefore worth keeping your eyes wide open and looking others deep in the eye.

40 Lamps and Sunglasses: Detection Theory, Controlitis and the Spotlight Test

What do cheats have in common? They all believe they can keep their cheating secret. What do cheats who get caught have in common? They wrongly believed that they could keep their cheating secret. They thought they could get away with it, but eventually they ran into trouble. Sometimes cheats are brought to light by unfortunate events. This happened to Barry, who worked as a parking attendant at a museum for 12 years. When he left at the age of 50, he had made it to a management position. So far no one suspected anything. Shortly after his departure, the parking lot takings increased significantly. Strange, because no more people were parking, and the charges had not risen. The investigation which followed led to Barry. He had found a loophole in the system. When he had been in service for approximately seven years, he came up with the idea of asking his colleagues to empty the parking meters, claiming that otherwise they would not work properly. The money picked up was to be delivered to him, so that he could pay it into the museum bank account. In reality he pocketed some of it. The sums he took increased over time, reaching 190,000 euros in total. Barry received a prison sentence and had to return the money.

Research by Donald Cressey among 300 managers and employees sentenced to prison for fraud shows that they all thought they could get away with it. Cressey's findings support "detection theory," which states that the chance of transgressions decreases as the chance of detection increases. When people contemplate behaving improperly, they take into account the likelihood of their actions coming to light. This means that the lower the chance of getting caught, the greater the chance of transgressions, as people show their true colors. According to this theory, a person's face is recognized in the light and his character in the dark.

Henry Schneider's undercover research shows how visibility affects behavior. In his experiment he offered 40 different garages a car to repair. This car had five evident and urgent defects: a loose battery cable, too little cooling fluid, a broken rear light, a leaky exhaust pipe, and a loose spark-plug wire. The car was otherwise in great shape.

In three-quarters of the garages an urgent problem was ignored because it was assumed that the owner didn't know he had a problem, and half the repairs charged for were for completely unnecessary repairs, because it was assumed that the customer would not know any better. Many invoices included a faulty starter motor, battery, radiator hose, thermostat, and water pump, when there was nothing wrong with these.

A mechanism for preventing this is transparency, as transparency gets transgressors sweating. It increases the perceived likelihood of getting caught, and it is perceived likelihood, not actual likelihood, that determines behavior. This is shown in research by Chen-Bo Zhong and colleagues. They carried out a series of experiments, discovering that people behave more egotistically and dishonestly not only in badly lit rooms, but also when wearing sunglasses. These circumstances make people feel more anonymous, but sunglasses have no affect on what others see. This is ostrich politics ("If I can't see, no one can"). If you are in doubt about a decision, you should ask yourself what you would do if everyone could see. This is known as the "front page test" or the "spotlight test." Does your behavior stand up to scrutiny?

Transparency in an organization can be promoted by having people work in teams (social control), setting matters down on paper, clearly assigning responsibilities, and carrying out checks. It is important not to go overboard: if everything is transparent, people will see nothing. Excessive checks, "controlitis," are costly, and can be interpreted as a sign of distrust. It raises the risk of people shifting their responsibilities on to the person doing the checking. Organizations also run the risk of what Daniel Wegner and colleagues call "ironic processes of control": when we focus too much on something, it is overemphasized, increasing the chance that it will go wrong. For example, they found evidence that when golfers focus too much on not doing one thing, they do exactly the opposite due to cognitive overload. In an organization with a strong focus on avoiding errors by means of checks, more errors will occur due to the focus on avoiding them. It is therefore important to know when to relax and let go.

Creating transparency is crucial for increasing the perceived chance of being caught and preventing transgressions. With enough light people will not feel they can hide. So key questions for organizations are whether there are enough lamps and whether the management sets a shining example.

41 Deceptive Appearances: Moral Self-Fulfillment and the Compensation Effect

One of the messages of the previous chapters is that we must use our eyes properly. However, this is easier said than done. There are all kinds of ways in which our view can be clouded. We can be wrong about an organization or person who does many good things, giving a great deal to good causes or putting in a great deal of extra work, for instance. We are naturally inclined to generalize the apparent goodness, and to view the whole organization or person as good. This is called the "halo effect." Organizations and individuals can make use of this, on purpose or subconsciously, setting others on the wrong track. The mechanism behind this is known as "moral self-fulfillment." People have a self-image which they wish to fulfill, as we saw in earlier chapters. Immoral or bad behavior threatens this image, so that they feel the need to compensate: a child who has been mischievous subsequently exhibits pro-social behavior. We use our good deeds to redress the moral balance. Laudable behavior can be motivated by previous reprehensible behavior. So when someone behaves well, do not simply assume that all is in order. The greatest philanthropist can also be the greatest offender.

This compensation effect also works in the opposite direction: when people feel their moral balance is "in credit," they feel this gives them the right to bad or immoral behavior. Today's moral behavior can lead to immoral behavior in the future ("I've kept to the speed limit so long, now I'm justified in driving faster"). Research by Nina Mazar and Chen-Bo Zhong shows that consumers who have just bought sustainable products lie and steal more than consumers who have bought the standard versions. Good behavior today is no guarantee of good behavior in the future. According to the theory of self-fulfillment, in fact, it opens the way to less good behavior in the future.

The compensation effect serves as a warning that we should not indiscriminately assume that a company which behaves responsibly toward customers, for example, does the same with other stakeholders. It is more likely that a company excelling and at the forefront in a particular area lags behind in another area. A company which makes intensive efforts to promote human rights may be fiddling the books, and one which works hard for the environment might be exploiting its own personnel.

There is another area where we risk being misled: people believe that they can tell from a person's appearance whether they are lying. We tend to think that integrity can be read in a person's face. Recent research shows that more than 50 percent of western populations believe that clean-shaven men are more honest than men with a beard. This explains why relatively few chairmen of boards grow beards. People also believe that external cleanliness coincides with integrity. John Stewart's research shows that good-looking men received lighter punishments for the same offences than less attractive men. Research in fact shows time and again that people are unable or barely able to tell from a person's appearance whether they are lying. In the experiment described in Chapter 2 parents were required to say whether their child had lied about looking at the toy. The parents' guesses as to whether their children had lied were no better than chance. Even parents cannot tell whether their children are telling the truth or lying. And these experiments only looked at *intentional* lies. People often think they are telling the truth when they lie, as we saw in Chapter 37, making it all the more difficult to separate the wheat from the chaff. Still, don't give up hope just yet. Although some people are better than others at lying, it appears that it is not so much our eyes we should be using as our ears. Aiden Gregg and his team subjected participants of their experiment to a special lie detector test.

The participants were required to reply to questions on a computer screen as quickly as possible. For some questions they were told to be honest, and for others to lie. The computer system recorded how long it took for the participants to give their answers. The results showed that 85 percent of the participants took more time to lie than to tell the truth. Giving an honest answer took 1.2 seconds on average. When entering a lie, participants took 50 percent longer. According to the researchers, telling a lie takes longer because it demands more complex activities in the brain.

On the one hand, research shows that liars need more time to formulate their lies. On the other hand, it has also been shown that liars say less and use fewer details. They say less because that way they run less risk of slipping up. And they recount fewer details because it is more difficult to make them up, and because it is easier to make a mistake with details than with vague, general statements.

It also turns out that, although truth may endure, the memory of a liar lingers on. A substantial body of experimental research shows that liars are remembered longer. They are more dangerous to our well-being, so make more of a mark on our brains. People also talk about liars a great deal in order to warn others, so that their names are more frequently activated in our brains and stick. That's why liars usually end up paying the price for their dishonesty.

42 Perverse Effects of Transparency: Moral Licensing and the Magnetic Middle

Transparency has become a magic word. As long as things are transparent, all is well, because transparency purifies and corrects. For this reason organizations often publicize their financial and social achievements, the composition and origin of their products, and their top salaries. Managers and employees should be open about their additional jobs, the gifts they receive, and the shares they own. Transparency, however, is not unequivocally beneficial: it has a dark side. This chapter discusses two ways in which transparency can perversely affect moral behavior, which we should guard against.

Research by Daylian Cain and colleagues sheds light on one negative effect of transparency. Their research was directed at experts and the information they provide about possible conflicts of interest in their advice to customers. For example, a mortgage adviser might receive a higher commission from one mortgage provider than another, or a doctor might expect better remuneration from one pharmaceutical company than another for the medicine he prescribes to his patient. People publish such conflicts of interest with the aim of preventing bias and prejudice. The expert will be more cautious about providing biased advice if he realizes that the customer is aware of his interest. To find out if this was really the case, Cain and colleagues came up with the following experiment.

The study centered on a glass bowl containing a number of small coins. The participants were assigned the role of an adviser or valuer. The adviser was required to research how many pennies were in the bowl and write a report. He was permitted to do whatever he wanted, apart from taking the coins out of the bowl and counting them one by one. The valuer, seated in another room, then received the report, and was also required to guess how many pennies were in the bowl, with the difference that the bowl was placed at a greater distance and the valuer had only ten seconds to make the estimation. The report by the adviser was therefore a welcome support.

The experiment played out over six rounds. The researchers varied the adviser's reward and the extent to which this was made known to the valuer. The average value of the bowl over the six rounds was 18.16 dollars. When the adviser was paid according to how well the valuer estimated the content, he advised that there were 16.48 dollars in the bowl on average. In this situation (where the adviser's interest ran parallel to that of the valuer), the adviser appeared to undervalue the bowl. When the adviser's pay rose the more the valuer guessed, without the valuer knowing how the adviser would be paid, he advised 20.16 dollars on average. In this conflict of interests (the higher the valuer's estimate, the less he would receive and the more the adviser would get) the adviser overvalued the bowl. What happened when the adviser's conflict of interests was made public? Contrary to expectations, the sum he advised did not drop, but in fact rose to an average of 24.16 dollars.

In this experiment publicizing conflicts of interest led to even greater distortion of the advice. All this when transparency about conflicts of interest was thought to lead to increased caution in giving biased advice. The opposite effect was caused by the fact that the advisers anticipated the reaction of the valuers when they were informed of the conflict of interest. The advisers expected the valuers to adjust the advice downwards, if they knew that the advisers would benefit from a high estimation. Anticipating this adjustment, the advisers raised their estimate even higher. The valuers appeared to discount this conflict of interests because it was difficult for them to predict what effect the conflict would have on the advice. The average estimation, in the situation in which the conflict of interest was made known, was 1.33 dollars higher than when the conflict of interest was unknown.

There is another explanation for the findings. The researchers call this "moral licensing." When the conflict of interest was known to the valuer and acknowledged by the adviser, transparency made the conflict appear less problematic, as if it had been agreed upon, and the adviser felt he had approval to give prejudiced advice. Transparency led the adviser to shift his responsibility to the valuer. As a result the adviser earned more and the valuer less.

Publicizing information can therefore have perverse effects. The adviser and valuer experiment shows that those who supply information can profit at the cost of the recipients. It is therefore important to be alert to such effects when creating transparency. When transparency is seen as a license ("As long as it's known, that's fine"), this undermines the ethics of the information provider. We see this in various areas. As long as salaries are transparent, it does not matter how high they are; as long as ingredients and risks are visible on the product packaging, the product is acceptable, even if it is full of junk and a health risk; as long as the information appears in a contract or report, it's up to the reader to decide what he does with it. As far as the information provider is concerned, he has fulfilled his responsibilities.

It is important not only to view ethics as something *procedural*, centering solely on transparency, but also as something *substantial*. Not all conflicts of interest should be permitted just because they are communicated. Not all gifts received are acceptable just because they have been made public. It is also important to regulate the content: what are responsible salaries, products, and contracts? If we have no answer, then we cannot communicate well, as we lack the ability to distinguish relevant information from irrelevant. Excessive communication is often a sign that the provider does not know his responsibilities. As the experiment above shows, he is also rewarded for this.

There is a second perverse effect of transparency: transparency is often created to gage, compare, and give feedback on performance or behavior, with the aim of improvement. It is supposed to lead us to drive one another's standards upwards, but this is not always the case, as established by Wesley Schultz and colleagues.

For their research they received permission from 290 households in California to measure their energy consumption on a weekly basis. The researchers took a reading and sent out cards to the owners stating their own energy consumption compared to the average for the neighborhood. As hoped and expected, in the following weeks energy consumption by those above the average decreased. They were aware that they used more than average, and that it was possible to use less. Energy consumption fell in this group by an average of 5.7 percent. But there was another group: the households who had heard that their consumption was *below* average. Here the opposite effect was observed: they were aware that they were below the average, and had the impression that they were perhaps being overly strict in their use of energy. In this group energy consumption rose by an average of 8.6 percent.

The researchers attributed this to what they called the "magnetic middle": people who differ from the norm, whether they are above or below, are pulled toward the middle. It is therefore important to watch out when communicating information of any kind within and outside organizations, whether it relates to productivity, absence through sickness, environmental effects, efficiency, damage, or customer satisfaction. Averages are soon seen as the norm. Employees, departments, and organizations who do better than the norm may be encouraged to make less effort.

Fortunately this does not mean that it is therefore better not to publicize any figures at all. If figures are accompanied by an injunctive norm, this helps keep this perverse effect in check. When Wesley Schultz and colleagues used "emoticons" in their feedback to the households (sad faces for big consumers and smiley faces for users who remained below the average), energy usage among high consumers fell by 5 percent, while low users remained at the same level. In this way transparency led to happy faces all round. So the challenge for organizations is to create transparency in such as way that it leads to happy faces.

Factor 6: Openness

In the previous section we saw that it is important that people in an organization have a clear view of their own behavior and that of others. Looking yourself in the eye is a way of promoting desirable behavior, both literally and figuratively. It is important to create transparency, without going over the top, so that people do not shirk their responsibilities or misjudge their own behavior.

There is a sixth factor which influences behavior in organizations: openness. This relates to the freedom people have to discuss opinions, feelings, dilemmas, and transgressions at work.

The next four chapters discuss several experiments which illustrate the meaning of openness. Chapter 43 explains the importance of sharing dilemmas in organizations. Chapter 44 shows that openness is often suppressed within groups, and there is a tendency toward conformity. Chapter 45 explains that freedom to express grievances prevents thoughts being suppressed and people acting improperly. In Chapter 46 we examine why people are slower to intervene in emergencies when there are more witnesses.

43 A Problem Shared is a Problem Halved: Communication Theory

Organizations enter the danger zone when dilemmas cannot be discussed, but are dismissed as a sign of weakness, lack of independence and indecision, as a cause of delay, vagueness, and discord. It is black or white; there is no space for shades of grey. "As an organization we should keep things clear and simple," so the thinking goes. However, going over complex questions together can be advantageous. This is shown in a study carried out by Kurt Lewin, one of the founders of social psychology, in the 1940s.

Lewin wanted to know how a change in eating pattern could best be implemented. He compared the effectiveness of lectures and group discussions. In both cases the same information was communicated regarding the importance of the new eating pattern and practical guidance for preparing meals. The only difference was that people in the discussion groups had the chance to discuss the pros and cons of the diet. Lewin noted that the effect of the lectures was quite limited, whereas the discussion groups worked much better. Furthermore the effect of the discussion groups did not wane with time, whereas that of the lectures faded. In the discussion groups participation appeared more effective than individual instructions. This excluded the possibility that the effect was caused by the amount of attention each person received. Lewin concluded that the opportunity to discuss norms and goals in a group was a critical factor in achieving the desired behavior.

Other studies have also demonstrated the importance of communal discussions to, for example, saving energy or combating theft at work. The important thing is always face-to-face interaction with people who serve as reference points, such as friends, neighbors, colleagues, or managers. All these findings support communication theory, which states that people learn from one another by discussing issues: they come to a better understanding of one another and their environment, and are more motivated to live up to expectations and comply with mutually agreed terms.

Dilemmas are situations in which those involved are unclear about what is expected of them. There are pros and cons: "As an employee can I take surplus goods home? It's a waste to throw it away, but I run the risk of being accused of theft." Discussion of these questions reveals potential conflict between different norms, or points where norms are insufficiently defined. Discussion also highlights the risks of wrong choices. For instance, if people can take surplus goods home, this increases the risk that they will intentionally over purchase. Discussion may prevent taboos and moral blindness, as people feel obliged to contribute and place themselves in one another's shoes, especially when dilemmas raise widely differing opinions within a group. The following experiment by Charles Lord and colleagues shows that people who are compelled to consider different viewpoints reach better decisions.

Participants were asked whether they were for or against the death penalty. They were then required to read four texts in an hour: two short summaries of empirical studies on the death penalty, reaching opposing conclusions as to its effectiveness, and more detailed two-page descriptions of each of the studies.

The participants were divided into three groups. Participants of the first group were asked to read the studies with an open mind and put themselves in the position of an independent lawyer. Participants of the second group were instructed to ask themselves at every step whether they would make the same judgment as to the quality of the research if it had shown the opposite results. The third group was the control, and received no specific instructions.

Participants already in favor of the death penalty in the control group appeared to be even more convinced of its advantages after reading the materials. The same applied to participants who were against the death penalty. The same information left them all more convinced of their original point of view. The same effect was observed in the group instructed to examine the studies without prejudice. This instruction had no effect whatsoever. The instruction to consider the opposite result, however, was effective: whether participants were for or against the death penalty, the information did not make them more convinced than they already were. Due to the instruction to consider the opposite, they were aware of their possible prejudice when processing the information. Because this group had processed the information in a genuinely unprejudiced manner, the foundation for their viewpoints improved.

In Lord's research the participants were left to themselves to come to a decision. The advantage of discussing dilemmas in groups is that it can lead to shared insight and mutual understanding: the group knows more than its individual members. Many experiments also show that participation in decision making leads to greater commitment and enjoyment in implementing decisions, even when this relates to difficult activities or really horrible tasks, such as eating worms. Just questioning one another increases levels of commitment. Various studies show that a simple question can change behavior. For example, when people are asked the day before elections whether they are planning to vote, this increases the chance that they will vote by 25 percent. If people are asked whether they are planning on buying a car in the next six months, this increases the chance of their buying a car by 35 percent.

The conclusion phase of a discussion is crucial; this is the phase in which agreements are made. Prior discussions resulting in firm agreements make people feel able to confront one another about their behavior. A large body of research illustrates the importance of giving people a choice and allowing them to commit. When salespeople send customers a confirmation form to sign, this significantly reduces the number of cancellations. Allowing people to actively agree to the outcome of a discussion increases the effect this has on their behavior. *Strike while the iron's hot.*

It is essential for organizations to create a culture in which dilemmas can be discussed. This can bring radical change, especially in organizations in which *money talks*, and all else is silent. Establishing this openness to discussion means more than just making it a fixed point on the agenda of meetings and appraisals. Of course it is good to call attention to it regularly, but it is particularly important that people are open to discussing sensitive issues at the moments when decisions are made. A problem shared is a problem halved; the process demonstrates people's willingness to speak up and to listen to one another.

44 What You See Is not What You Say: Group Pressure and Conformity

Homo sapiens non urinat in ventum: a wise man does not piss into the wind. The purport of this pseudo Latin saying is that a sensible person would stand with his back to the wind, otherwise he'd get a wet suit. This wisdom is often taken to heart: for the sake of peace we swallow criticism and blow with the wind. We move with the group to avoid being a nuisance. Even if we don't agree with something, we keep quiet, otherwise it would damage the solidarity of the group.

Conformity, adjusting to the opinion of the group, is good, up to a point. We comply with traffic regulations and stand in line for the check-out. In this way we show respect for the rules. Conformity also stems from people's need to belong and be connected with others. When we fail to fit in, we run the risk of being excluded or cast out, ending up on the sidelines without influence. But how far does conformity stretch? Would we even close our eyes to abuses to fit in with the group? Solomon Asch wanted to prove that people can come to an independent judgment on self-evident issues, without needing someone else's opinion. He designed the following, now famous experiment.

In each round seven people were invited to take part in an eye test. They were seated next to one another at a large table. The group was given two cards to look at, one with one line and the other with three lines of different lengths. The participants were required to say which line on the second card was the same length as the line on the first card, giving their answers out loud. In fact only one of the seven participants was really a subject. The rest had received instructions in advance. Asch wanted to know to what extent this person's opinion would be determined by that of the others. Asch therefore always placed the subject sixth in line at the table, so that he heard the answers of five others before being invited to give his own opinion.

Initially nothing out of the ordinary occurred, the whole group giving the same answer as the subject. But after 12 rounds all the other partici-pants gave answers which were clearly wrong. Would the subject continue to follow his own observations, or would he adjust to fit in with the group? Asch expected the majority of subjects not to state something that was clearly wrong.

Contrary to expectation, in the following 12 rounds 75 percent of the subjects gave at least one wrong answer. At least half of the subjects answered wrong in more than half of the rounds and 5 percent gave the wrong answer every time, following the group's opinion, instead of saying what they could see with their own eyes.

Curious as to their motives, Asch interviewed the subjects after the experiment. Those who had conformed in most cases admitted that they had seen the correct answer, but that they had gone along with the group out of uncertainty ("If everyone sees it that way, it must be true"), or because they did not want to place themselves outside the group. Many of the subjects who did stick by their own opinion also stated that they felt under pressure during the experiment.

Asch's research has been repeated more than a hundred times, with the repeated finding that 20–40 percent of subjects follow a false group opinion. The experiments show that social pressure can lead people to say things which are clearly false in their own eyes. Despite disagreeing, we conform to the dominant opinion. People are like sheep and will follow the flock.

If we extend these results to the workplace, we find that circumstances are no more conducive to independent opinion-forming. Asch's experiment looked at something evident and demonstrable. In practice the issues at stake are often unclear and ambiguous, making it all the more difficult to hold a different opinion. Asch's experiment also looked at a group of strangers, with whom the subjects had no connection. In an organization, however, it is more important to be valued by those around you. You work closely with these people and your future is bound up with them, increasing the social pressure. In the experiment the subject of the question was trivial and nothing important was at stake, but in the workplace major interests hang in the balance. All this makes it more difficult to deviate from the group opinion in a real life situation.

It is therefore essential to create a culture in which there is the freedom to express different opinions, in which dissenters are heard and people with a unique voice are valued. One divergent opinion can make a big difference. Follow-up research by Asch shows that when the group contains someone with a different opinion, conformism among the subjects drops by a factor of three.

One method of preventing conformism is to use an anonymous, written voting system for decision making. Asch's experiment showed that when the participants were required to put their answers down on paper (with the others stating their answers out loud), conformity halved to an average of 12.5 percent.

Taking decisions in small groups, however, turns out not to be a solution for preventing conformity. Asch and other researchers found that although the tendency to conform increases with the size of the group, this effect does not intensify beyond three people. Only in pairs is the tendency significantly reduced.

Getting one's suit wet is no good for anyone, but drowning among the masses and losing one's identity and integrity is worse. It is therefore crucial to draw the line in going along with the group and swallowing the truth.

45 Explaining, Speaking Out, and Letting off Steam: Pressure Build-Up Under Thought Suppression

Managers are not always in a position to save the day and make everyone happy; sometimes they must make painful, radical decisions, when it becomes necessary to let people or activities go, drastically reduce costs, cut away parts of the organization, or make fundamental strategic changes. In such situations there is a risk of becoming bogged down in conflicts and resistance, deadlines and budget overruns, and losing one's credibility as a manager.

Much can be said for the claim that no real change can be made without pain, and that pain is always paired with resistance. A manager should not strive for popularity. Leadership often means going against the current. This does not necessarily mean that the manager must ride roughshod over the feelings of personnel and push on through with decisions in spite of them. The extent to which employees are taken into account in painful decisions determines the extent to which those decisions are accepted and have the desired effect.

Jerald Greenberg wanted to know the effects of painful decisions on the ethics of employees. He was curious in particular as to the effect of the way in which the decision was communicated. He found a company that was willing to participate in his research. At this company the board had found it necessary to take a painful decision.

The company had three factories where small mechanical parts were made for the automobile and aircraft industries. Due to the loss of two large contracts, the board was forced to reduce labor costs by 15 percent at the head office and two of the three factories. This was to be achieved without redundancies. In the two factories it was decided that the decision would be communicated in two different ways, so that Greenberg could compare the effects. The third factory, where no pay reduction was taking place, functioned as the control group. In order to put the effects into context, Greenberg collected various information, such as the number of thefts from the warehouse by employees, from 10 weeks before the pay cut until 10 weeks afterwards. Before the cut, theft in all three factories was the same, at 3.7 percent of stock. In the factory where no cut was made, the control group, this percentage remained the same in all weeks, but what happened in the other two factories?

In the first factory the board decided to call the employees together to inform them of their decision. All employees were assembled and the vice chairman informed them that a salary reduction of 15 percent would take effect from the following week and was predicted to last 10 weeks. The vice chairman also explained the reason for this measure, the cancellation of two large contracts. The board did several things right here: they informed the staff, in person and in the presence of everyone involved, giving concrete figures and reasons for the decision. However, if we look at theft in this factory, then it appears that the morals of the employees went sharply downhill. Theft rose by almost 150 percent to 8.9 percent. A survey among the employees showed that they felt insufficiently informed. Satisfaction with their salaries dropped by 40 percent. Could things have gone better? Greenberg looked at the second factory.

Here too all employees were informed. In this case it was not the vice chairman who came to break the news, but the chairman himself. The meeting lasted a full hour and a half. Employees were also told that the board seriously regretted the situation, even though it did avoid the need for redundancies. He guaranteed that the same reduction applied to everyone, with no exceptions. With visual aids the chairman gave a detailed explanation of the problem of the stagnation in cash flow and how the salary reduction could fill this gap. The employees received a guarantee that the reduction in salary would last a maximum of 10 weeks. After the chairman's presentation, all employees were given an hour to ask questions, during which time the chairman emphasized his personal regret over the situation.

Even this did not prevent increased theft, but in this case, the increase was only 50 percent, instead of 150 percent, as in the first factory. The survey also showed that employee satisfaction about salaries and salary information was unharmed, in contrast to the first factory.

In the second factory a couple of aspects had therefore worked out better than in the first, which offers clues as to the way to communicate painful decisions. The chairman made it known that he personally found the situation painful, gave a detailed explanation of the decision and a clear endpoint, and offered the freedom to ask questions. It may be obvious, but it is not always followed up in practice. Research into the effects of the financial and economic crisis shows that one in three employees takes a new job if the opportunity arises, because they feel they have been dishonestly or unethically treated by top management as a result of lack of open communication. The same research shows that top managers feel they have taken into account the consequences of their decisions for the ethical behavior of their personnel. The fact that almost half of employees state that unethical behavior on the work floor increased as a result of the lack of communication from the top over the decision is in line with Greenberg's earlier findings.

One of the strengths of the approach in the second factory was that employees were given the freedom to let off steam and have their say. There is abundant literature showing that when people feel they must suppress their feelings, they look for another outlet. The more their own thoughts must be suppressed, the greater the pressure to think about them. People are then unable to let go, become stressed and tired (suppression costs energy), and let rip at the most inappropriate moments or even take the law into their own hands. Employees can, for example, end up stealing more out of a feeling of "corrective justice." It is therefore always better to allow freedom to express frustrations and ask questions. It is not simply a matter of providing a listening ear, but also of asking employees the right questions, encouraging and challenging them to bring the suppressed feelings and bottled up frustrations to the surface. The deeper something is hidden away, the deeper one must dig and the less people are able to do this for themselves. In the end such an open attitude is good not only for the health of the company, but also the health of the employees themselves. Research has shown that open people run less health risks than those who bottle up their problems.

46 Blow the Whistle and Sound the Alarm: The Bystander Effect and Pluralistic Ignorance

You notice a colleague cutting corners, the organization selling substandard products, nepotism, and abuse of power running riot. Time to talk about it? It is the norm in many organizations to confront undesirable behavior, at least in theory. Anyone who sees a transgression should raise the alarm and challenge the offender or tip off the management. Enron had this expressly set out in its code of conduct. The company even handed out notepads with a quote by Martin Luther King: "Our lives begin to end the day we become silent about things that matter."

People who witness a misdemeanor or incident can react in three possible ways, variously described as exit, voice, loyalty, or flight, fight, freeze. People can walk on by or run away; they can make their voice heard, help out or take action in some other way; or they can remain rooted to the spot, passively looking on. A substantial body of empirical research shows that employees are often aware of transgressions within organizations but do not intervene. They stand and look on or go about their business, like the priest and the Levite in Chapter 26. In that case time pressure was the excuse, but an experiment by John Darley and Bibb Latané suggests that there is another explanation for people's failure to act as they should.

The participating students were lured to the lab under the pretext of an interview about their personal difficulties with student life. Due to the personal nature of the subject matter, each participant was placed in a separate room, so that they were unable to see one another, and the group conversation took place over an intercom system. What the participant in each round did not know was that he or she was the sole subject, and that the others were part of the experimental set-up. The leader of the discussion explained the goal of the session and then withdrew, because sensitive matters were to be discussed.

In the first round all participants were given the chance to introduce themselves and say a bit about their problems. In the second round everyone responded one by one to what the others had said. Suddenly one "participant" whose turn it was to speak became unwell. The subject heard the participant begin to stammer and ask for help. He stuttered something about an epileptic fit and that he was going to die. Then there was a choking sound and it went completely silent. What would the subject do? The subject was not able to talk over the intercom, because only the person whose turn it was to speak was able to make the switch. The subject was therefore unable to communicate with the victim, or with the other participants. The subject also did not know what the other participants were doing.

When the subjects were told in advance that only one other person was taking part in the session, the victim, 85 percent of the subjects acted within two minutes. When the session consisted of three participants, this percentage dropped to 62 percent. With five it dropped to 31 percent. Reaction speeds also slowed: the larger the group, the slower the reactions of those who acted at all. Although only one person in a group needed to act, it seemed that the bigger the group the lower the chance of the victim receiving help. In groups of two or three participants, 50 percent of the victims received help within 45 seconds. In groups of six participants none did.

According to Darley and Latané, the passivity exposed here does not come from indifference. Many of the passive subjects were clearly upset. As in Stanley Milgram's experiment (see Chapter 18), they sweated, their hands shook, and they looked around them uneasily. Their passivity was caused by the "bystander effect": the more witnesses there are, the fewer people act. For instance, the more people stand on the shore watching someone drown, the less likely anyone is to offer help. The more people see a fire, theft, or act of violence, the less likely anyone is to call the police. The more people in an organization witness a misdemeanor, the less likely it is that someone will raise the alarm or blow the whistle.

The reasons for this passivity can be are threefold. First, the bigger the group, the greater the uncertainty as to responsibilities. This is especially so if there is no hierarchy to a group of witnesses. The bigger the group, the easier it is for people to hide behind others and shift their responsibility ("They didn't do anything either"). The more people there are to take responsibility, the less people have a sense of their own responsibility. Second, there is a social effect: people look at what everyone else does. As long as others do nothing, the message is that passivity is the norm. There must be a reason that no one is doing anything. Perhaps the incident or transgression is less serious than it looks, or perhaps it's the victim's fault. When people look at one another like this, it becomes more difficult to break with this norm. Thirdly, people feel constrained from acting because this will be seen by the group and might be condemned. Fear of the accusation of having misunderstood the situation makes people reluctant to take action. These three reasons together are termed "pluralistic ignorance": because people don't know what others think, they come up with their own interpretation, leaving the group caught up in itself, unable to change the status quo.

This risk of "bystander inertia" is present in the workplace. The larger and more complex the organization, the easier it is to shift or shirk responsibilities. Organizations themselves can look at one another, waiting for another to tackle issues which affect the entire sector. As long as everyone is looking at someone else, nothing will actually happen. The problem will only grow.

The solution is to confront the situation, to break through the silence and passivity. This is not achieved by emphasizing the importance of such action on paper. Whistleblowing legislation and hotlines for abuses are effective, albeit to a limited extent. It is primarily a matter of instilling a culture in which everyone acknowledges and takes responsibility for acting when an incident takes place, or they have reason to suspect something. Some organizations state that all those aware of an incident share responsibility unless it is reported. Silence means consent. To prevent people holding their tongues, it is necessary to remove the fear that employees who misjudge the situation and take action unnecessarily will meet with reprisals. A feeling of safety is essential. In that respect organizations have an advantage: they are not separate individuals who have coincidentally come together in an experiment or to witness an incident in the street, but groups of people with a communal goal, bound together in long-term collaboration, which should make it easier to build up a sense of shared responsibility and openness. Shouldn't it?

Factor 7: Enforcement

In the previous section we saw that openness in an organization helps in addressing dilemmas and incidents, and preventing people from looking on passively or even running away when help is needed. In an insufficiently open organization less is learnt, encouraging group thinking and blindness to shortcomings, and people look for unethical ways of letting off steam. It is therefore important for organizations to create an open and protective work environment, in which people can talk about their feelings and dilemmas and raise criticism.

The seventh and final factor which effects behavior in organizations is enforcement. Enforcement is the extent to which people within the organization are valued and rewarded for exhibiting desired behavior and punished for undesirable behavior, and the extent to which they learn from mistakes, incidents, and accidents.

In the following five chapters, several experiments are discussed which illustrate the meaning of enforcement. Chapter 47 teaches the value of showing appreciation. Chapter 48 shows that people and organizations often think when a transgression takes place that a symbolic purge is sufficient, whereas what is actually needed is a thorough clean-up. Chapter 49 explains the positive effect of punishment, and the various risks associated with it. Chapter 50 goes into detail on the risks of penalties. Chapter 51, the final chapter on enforcement, explains the dangers of rewards and bonuses. Finally, Chapter 52 addresses the way the different factors influence people dealing with ethical dilemmas within organizations.

47 The Value of Appreciation: Compliments and the Midas Effect

In order to encourage people to do the right thing, you must reward them for it. Research shows that the more ethical behavior is rewarded in organizations, the more honest the actions of managers and employees. For that reason organizations increasingly incorporate ethical behavior, in terms of customer satisfaction, staff satisfaction, impact on the environment, social activities, and compliance with rules and regulations into their appraisal and reward systems. However, there are risks associated with this policy. One such risk is that incorporating it into the appraisal and reward process misses the point.

The process is often extremely complex: each role and level comprises a broad range of competencies, criteria, indicators, and targets. The evaluator must assign a score to each of these aspects each year and enter them into the system. The advantage of such a structure is that it is standardized and automated, so that employees know what criteria they are judged on, it can be applied fairly and the result is recorded. However, the standardization and automatization conceals the risk of the evaluation itself becoming mechanical and impersonal. The organization prides itself on its meticulous approach, but even the big earners still complain about a lack of appreciation. The evaluation becomes a mathematical exercise, which mainly takes place at a computer and in which personal appreciation is not expressed.

Appreciation is important, possibly the most important element of evaluation and reward. Whether people earn a lot or a little, are placed high or low in the organization, they all have a serious need to be appreciated, to feel that what they do is of value to others. When people feel appreciated, they have higher self-esteem, feel a stronger bond with the organization, and are more motivated to make an effort and create value. The effect of appreciation is illustrated in a study by Robert Kraut. He came up with the following experiment.

A collector for the American Heart Association went from door to door in different neighborhoods of the city of New Haven. When anyone donated the collector gave him a leaflet. In half of the cases the collector also said some words of appreciation: "You are a generous person. I wish more of the people I met were as charitable as you." To half of those who donated nothing, the collector said the following: "Let me just give you one of our leaflets anyway. We've been giving them to everyone, even people like you who are uncharitable and don't normally give to these causes." This was the first part of the experiment.

The second part followed approximately a week later. A collector called again, this time to collect money for multiple sclerosis. At each house the collector noted what was donated. Did the previous collector's reaction affect what people gave this time?

This was indeed the case: of those who had given money the first time and only received the leaflet, 47 percent gave again; of those who had also received words of appreciation, 62 percent gave again. And the sum given rose by as much as 70 percent! The reverse also appeared to apply: of the people who had given nothing and received a negative response, significantly fewer people gave compared with those who had given nothing but received no negative response.

This experiment illustrates the effect of appreciation: a few simple words can make people feel valued, rightly or wrongly, and therefore put in more, or indeed less effort. It is not only important *that* someone is valued, but also that it is emphasized *what* is valued. This shows which values are really important in the organization. But this is a difficult area. Things can go wrong with personal appreciation in organizations: by setting up an extensive appraisal and reward system, for example, the company runs the risk of missing the personal dimension. This cannot be programmed into the system, and depends on the communicative abilities of the evaluator.

Appreciation can be communicated in small ways: a remark, a moment's attention, a smile, a present or an email message can make a big difference. Even brief physical contact can work. April Crusco and Christopher Wetzel have shown that hairdressers who touch a client's palm or shoulder for 1.5 seconds receive 25 percent more in tips. This is known as the "Midas effect," named after King Midas from Greek mythology, who turned everything he touched to gold. When people feel touched (literally or figuratively), they change, figuratively, into gold. At the same time, we must take care not to touch one another too often or at the wrong moments. Research shows that when a man receives a pat on the shoulder or a pat on the back from a woman, he is more inclined to gamble money or make risky investments. So be careful when you have an important financial decision to make and someone touches you. Otherwise the gold could disappear like snow in the sun.

48 Washing Dirty Hands: Self-Absolution and the Macbeth Effect

Watch out for anyone who washes his hands immediately after a meeting, feels the need to take a shower or bath after work when no physical exertion was involved, or even visits a spa after taking major decisions. Why is this suspicious?

In many religions physical cleanliness is central and is coupled with spiritual and psychological purity. Christians are baptized with water, symbolizing the washing away of their sins, Hindus wash their bodies to purify their souls and Muslims wash before praying. Physical cleanliness is coupled with spiritual cleanliness. But does it really literally work that way? That sounds risky. After doing something unethical, figuratively getting our hands dirty, we can literally wash our hands and come out with a clean conscience! Chen-Bo Zhong and Katie Liljenquist carried out research into what they call the "Macbeth effect." In Shakespeare's play Lady Macbeth hopes to cleanse her conscience, after the treacherous murder of King Duncan, by washing the imagined blood from her hands, as if this could also wash away her crime. Zhong and Liljenquist came up with the following experiment.

Half of the participants were asked to think of an unethical act in the past and to describe the feelings this memory raised. The other half were asked to do the same with a good deed. The participants were subsequently tasked with finishing incomplete English words. These words could always be completed in multiple ways. "W**h" could be *wish* or *wash*, and "s**p" *soup* or *soap*, for example. People who had thought of an unethical deed, made 60 percent more cleaning-related words than participants of the other group. Clearly unethical behavior brings up associations with cleaning. But this was not the end of their experiment. The participants were offered a thank-you gift, and given a choice of a pen or a disinfectant wipe. In the control group, in which people had thought of something neutral before the experiment began, both objects were chosen with equal frequency. But in the group which had thought of something unethical, as much as 75 percent opted for the disinfectant wipe, whereas in the group which had thought of doing good the figure was only half this, at 37.5 percent.

According to Zhong and Liljenquist their research shows that people like to have a "clean" self-image. When this image is threatened, and people feel bad and "dirty," they literally seek to clean up their acts. This cleansing can happen spiritually or physically, because in our heads the two are interchangeable. Physical cleansing also cleanses the spirit, allowing us to wash away emotions such as disgust, regret, shame, guilt, embarrassment, and rage.

The danger is evident. If it is so easy to cleanse an unclean conscience, why would people feel it necessary to restore the damage, apologize, and learn from it? The disinfectant wipe effectively cleanses the conscience and ensures that we can get on with our day. That opens the door to repetition. Disinfectant wipes are nothing more than rags to wipe away the blood. Zhong and Liljenquist discovered this in a follow-up experiment: the same participants were asked to help someone in need. Of those who had not cleaned their hands with the disinfectant wipe, 74 percent helped; of the participants who had cleaned their hands, only 41 percent helped.

In other words, our colleagues' hand-washing may have been preceded by unsavory acts. It is also important to watch out for organizations that only clean superficially after a scandal, without undergoing a deeper cleansing process. The greater the scandal, the more intensive the cleaning should be. Siemens is a good example in this respect. The German manufacturer of products such as washing machines had paid bribes on a large scale. The cleansing of the company consisted of Siemens setting a goal only to do business in an honest manner from then on. The slogan read: "Only Clean Business is Siemens Business. Everywhere — Everybody — Every Time!" In order to make a clean sweep, all employees involved were treated harshly: the real rotten apples were eliminated. An ethics and compliance department was set up with 600 employees, the structure of the organization was changed, training programs were rolled out, new employees were required to sign Siemens' code of conduct, and compliance counted 17 percent toward managers' bonuses. Siemens' reputation and profits were considerably improved after this thorough cleanout.

So if an organization has dirty laundry, the question is which program to choose on the "washing machine": a short, energy-saving program or a long intensive wash?

49 Punishment Pitfalls: Deterrence Theory

Giuseppe, a hospital director, was suspended after sending personnel a memo telling them not to take cocaine during working hours. Giuseppe decided to send this memo after receiving various anonymous tip-offs about cocaine use by hospital personnel. He thought he was doing the right thing in communicating the policy clearly and therefore sent the memo to the entire staff. The regulators thought otherwise. They gave Giuseppe to understand that "the suspected use of cocaine in a hospital should certainly not be handled in this way." The director would have done better to focus his efforts on getting to the root of the problem, before working on prevention (a memo in any case being the weakest form of prevention).

It may be that few managers send such memos, but in some respects Giuseppe's action is not so unusual. Signs of transgression are regularly made light of or ignored by management. Around one-third of the American professional population in fact feel that their managers do not handle signs of transgression effectively.

"Deterrence theory" states that punishment is a condition for effective administration and regulation. Lack of punishment gives out the signal that transgressions are not so bad after all, at least not so bad as to be worth enforcing. This undermines the credibility of those who have established the policy and rules. What is this authority worth, after all, if it states how things should be done, and then fails to do anything when people take no notice? Does it believe in its policy? Does it believe in itself? This undermines the whole normative framework: if one rule is sanctioned and not another, this quickly leads to an idea of arbitrariness and class justice. The effectiveness of punishment is shown in the study by Fisman and Miguel on parking offenses by diplomats in New York discussed in Chapter 8.

When diplomatic immunity was removed in 2002, the number of parking penalties dropped by 98 percent.

Deterrence theory states that, in order to prevent things from going from bad to worse, it is important that the punishment be heavy, unequivocal, and immediate. If signs of abuse emerge, it is a matter of finding out the nature and context of the transgression, something which Giuseppe omitted to do, and taking the correct measures based on the facts. In all fairness, this is easier said than done, as the facts can often be set out and interpreted in various different ways. Research shows that people tend to underestimate the external factors which influence the behavior of the transgressor. The more serious the transgression, the more people tend to attribute malicious intent to the transgressor, even if it is clearly evident that the transgression is the result of environmental factors. Victims are particularly inclined to think that there is no such thing as coincidence. People judge transgressors they do not know well more harshly than those close to them. The description of the transgression also affects the judgment: people are less harsh in their judgments of fraudulent behavior if the company is described as having "a better reputation than a third of its competitors," compared to when the company has "a worse reputation than two-thirds of the competition." Even when the offence is the same.

Zero tolerance, a firm approach, harsh punishment; companies often announce resolute measures when they first open the can of worms. Sometimes you have to be cruel to be kind; but organizations should be careful not to hit too hard, because there are plenty of pitfalls. Severe punishments are no panacea. Even the death penalty's effectiveness is disputed. Some studies show that executions in fact lead to more murders, though there is no conclusive proof of this. Furthermore, the offender is not always affected by the seriousness of the penalty; think for instance of crimes of passion. Another point of concern is the time and energy it costs to keep a system of sanctions, with administration, supervision, monitoring, and enforcement in place. The more effort the system of sanctions demands, the greater the chance that attention will slip and the system will be applied less strictly. Research shows that confidence can subsequently drop to a level below the time before the sanctions were introduced. When establishing such a system, be aware that there is no way back. A third danger lies in the mechanism by which the more severe the punishment, the less the enforcers are prepared to confront offenders. More is at stake for the offender, so the enforcer must have clearer proof. The suspected offender's opposition will also be greater the more severe the punishment. This can give rise to a situation in which harsher punishments lead to greater tolerance for transgressions.

The fourth pitfall is probably the most important: research shows that, in order to achieve behavioral change, mild punishments are more effective than severe punishments. Elliot Aronson and Merrill Carlsmith carried out a famous study in this area.

Young children were permitted to pick out a favorite toy, and were then told that they were not allowed to play with it. One group was told that there would be a mild punishment for breaking the ban; the other group was told that there would be a severe punishment. The researcher then left the room, giving the children the opportunity to ignore the instruction. In all cases the children did as they were told. The next question was what the children would do if they were then told that they were allowed to play with the toy again. The results, as in many follow-up studies, showed that the children in the mild punishment situation were less inclined to play with their favorite toy than those in the severe punishment situation.

We can explain what happened on the basis of cognitive dissonance theory, discussed in Chapter 37: severe punishment serves as an external justification for the children not doing what they have been banned from doing. If the punishment is minor, the children need an internal justification to reduce their feeling of dissonance stemming from the tension between wanting to play and not playing. The children had to convince themselves that their favorite toy was actually not so attractive after all. This self-justification resulted in the children convincing themselves and a reduced preference for their favorite toy.

So the challenge for organizations is to punish where necessary, and to do so mildly where possible, in order to achieve the desired change in behavior. Unfortunately this advice comes too late for Giuseppe.

50 The Price of a Penalty: The Crowding-Out Effect

The lesson to take from the previous chapter is that one should be alert to the risks of severe punishment. Severe punishment can lead to people complying with the norm *because of the punishment*. The disadvantage of this is that as soon as the punishment is reduced or removed the old, undesirable behavior returns. And that's not all. Even mild punishments can have a negative effect, an effect which is not easy to repair. Research by Uri Gneezy and Aldo Rustichini shows how this works.

Gneezy and Rustichini carried out research at day-care centers in Israel. The management had a problem: the parents were supposed to pick up their children at four in the afternoon, but often arrived late, so that the staff had to wait. The managers decided to introduce a penalty. When a parent arrived more than 10 minutes late, 3 dollars extra per child was added to the monthly bill of 380 dollars. The penalty was introduced at six of the ten day-care centers. The four day-care centers where the penalty was not introduced acted as a control group, so that the changes could be compared. In these four day-care centers the percentage of late parents remained the same. The managers hoped that the penalties would solve the problems at the six day-care centers where they were applied. Unfortunately, instead of the number of late parents dropping, it actually grew. In no time at all, the percentage had actually doubled.

In order to understand what happened here, we must first investigate why people pick up their children on time. They do this for moral reasons ("Punctuality is the norm," "A promise is a promise"), or social reasons ("The staff, other parents and my own children will disapprove if I'm late and approve if I'm on time"). Introducing a penalty added an economic reason. One more reason to be on time, you might think. In fact the opposite was the case. The economic motive wiped out the other motives: the punishment put arriving late in an economic context, making people think in a calculating way. Arriving on time was an economic consideration: "Shall I pay the price of the penalty for being late, so that I can finish my work first?" This placed moral and social motives in the background. This is why this is called the "crowding-out effect." The penalty meant that the parents could buy off their guilt ("After all, I'm paying for it, aren't I?").

The crowding-out effect explains all kinds of behavior in organizations. A penalty for handing in borrowed items late means that the items are returned even later. A penalty for damaged equipment leads to more equipment breaking down. A penalty for equipment that disappears leads to more being taken. Organizations too can come to think this way: a penalty for breaking a rule or contract becomes an economic consideration, instead of a moral or social issue. Instead of people asking themselves whether something is permissible or obligatory, it becomes all about the chance of getting caught, the chance of being convicted, the size of the penalty and the measures to be taken to minimize all of these. When introducing punishments, it is therefore essential to consider the possible negative effects on people's moral and social motivations, and the possible end results. Gneezy and Rustichini's research shows that on balance penalties can have a negative effect.

The managers of the group of day-care centers also realized this. They therefore decided to get rid of the penalty. Unfortunately this did nothing to change the number of parents who turned up late and continued to do so. For this group, economic motives had permanently replaced moral and social motives. The parents could now arrive late without paying a penalty *and* without a guilty conscience. Experimenting with punishment can cost you dear.

51 The Corrupting Influence of Rewards and Bonuses: The Overjustification Effect

The crowding-out effect applies to reward as well as punishment. Rewards appeal to economic motives and suppress moral and social motives. Classic research by David Greene and colleagues shows how extrinsic motives can displace intrinsic motives.

Teachers introduced their students to four new types of calculation. Over a block of 13 days they recorded how much time the students spent on these questions. In the first block the children spent around 18 minutes per day on the sums. In the second block the teachers introduced a reward: the longer the children worked on the calculations, the more points they were awarded. The expectation was that the students would now spend more time on the questions. This was indeed the case, with an average of 25 minutes per day spent on the calculations in this second block. The reward was therefore effective. What would happen if the reward was removed? When the teachers did this, the time spent reduced. Logical enough, since the time increased with the reward. But the time spent was now far below the initial time: at the end of the third block it was just 5 minutes.

The students' intrinsic motives had been replaced by extrinsic motives; initially the students did the calculations because they enjoyed it and wanted to learn. The extrinsic motivation was an additional motivation. This led to the "overjustification effect." People tend to see their behavior as motivated by attractive extrinsic reasons, and underestimate the extent to which it is guided by intrinsic reasons. This makes people less intrinsically motivated, as becomes clear when the extrinsic motivation is removed. Hundreds of studies show that rewards have a considerable negative effect on people's intrinsic motivation, even when the rewards are attached to performance.

Another mechanism is at work which explains why extrinsic motives lead to reduced intrinsic motivation. People who are intrinsically motivated will be less motivated to exhibit the desired behavior after the introduction of rewards because others may now think they are doing so for their own benefit. Research shows that the introduction of modest financial compensation for blood donors led to half of the donors dropping out. A study in Switzerland showed that when the government offered citizens financial compensation for the storage of nuclear waste in their area, half of the citizens withdrew their consent. The intrinsic motive for contributing to a social problem (a shortage of blood or the need for storage of nuclear waste) disappeared.

Rewards are also risky because they remind us of unpleasant things we were forced to do. This begins at a young age, when children are rewarded for leaving an empty plate (for instance with dessert or being allowed to leave the table sooner), for doing housework and tidying their room. This leads us to associate rewards with activities for which we are not intrinsically motivated. By coupling rewards to work, work is associated with boredom, monotony and annoyance, even if this is not really the case. Rewards are only effective when it comes to activities which people do not wish to do, and for which they cannot be intrinsically motivated.

Of course organizations which attempt to appeal to the intrinsic motivation of underpaid employees are missing the point. The question is *how* people see their reward. Is a bonus seen as an extra reward? Or as the motivation to put in the effort? Another point is how many criteria are desirable for determining the reward and possible bonus: the more criteria the organization takes into consideration, the clearer it is for employees that several criteria are important for success. However, the more criteria are considered, the greater the risk that anything not included is seen as unimportant. For this reason in many organizations in recent years the number of criteria for a bonus has increased substantially, sometimes to as many as 25. If the organization's management needs so many criteria, it should stop and ask itself whether it is a sign of weakness not to be able to motivate employees intrinsically. Clearly the intrinsic motivation of employees will not be improved by so many performance criteria.

52 The Heinz Dilemma: Levels of Moral Development

The way in which people deal with an ethical dilemma reveals their level of moral development. This level can be inferred from the arguments people use. Lawrence Kohlberg developed a model for this, which combines a number of insights from the previous chapters.

Kohlberg wondered where the difference in morality lies between the man in the street and role models such as Mahatma Gandhi and Albert Einstein. In order to research this question, he presented children and adults with moral dilemmas. The best-known dilemma is the "Heinz dilemma."

Somewhere in Europe a woman is dying of a rare form of cancer. There is a new medicine, which the doctors believe might save her life. The treatment contains radium and was recently discovered by a pharmacist in the same city. The preparation process is expensive, but the pharmacist is asking ten times as much. He paid 5,000 euros for the radium and is asking 50,000 euros for a small dose of the medicine. Heinz, the sick woman's husband, goes to everyone he knows trying to scrape together the money. He only manages to get 25,000 euros, half of what he needs. Heinz tells the pharmacist that his wife is dying and asks him to sell the treatment at a lower price, or to allow him to pay the rest later. The pharmacist replies, "No, I discovered the medicine and I want to earn money from it." Heinz becomes desperate, breaks into the pharmacy and steals the medicine.

What do you think of Heinz's actions? Are they acceptable or not? And why? Is it acceptable because the woman expects this of him, or because everyone has a right to life? Or is it unacceptable, because Heinz should obey the law? Kohlberg collected the participants' answers and observed that they could be divided into three successive levels of moral argumentation. The point was not the choice itself, but the justification the participant gave. The three levels are the "preconventional level" (where people are focused on self-interest and extrinsic reward and punishment), the "conventional level" (where people do what others expect), and the "postconventional level (where people come to a decision on the basis of principles they have chosen themselves). Each level consists of two stages.

Stage 1 of the first level is characterized by the avoidance of punishments such as those imposed by the authorities. Anything for which there is a punishment is bad; anything with no punishment, or even a reward, is good. For example, "Heinz should not steal the medicine because he will end up in prison and that would mean that he is a bad person" or "Heinz should steal the medicine, because it is worth much less than what the pharmacist is asking. Heinz has even offered to pay, so he won't be punished."

At stage 2 of the preconventional level, the stage of self-interest, people do not allow themselves to be guided purely by punishment by an authority, because they realize there are different sides to a dilemma: different people have different opinions. Heinz may think that it is good to steal the medicine, and the pharmacist may disagree. Because everything is relative, one is free to follow self-interest, although it is often useful to take the interests of others into account. This is taking reciprocity as the basis: morality as a deal. Punishment is not seen as determining what is good or bad, but as a risk factor. In this case Heinz should steal the medicine because, "he will be much happier if he rescues his wife, even if he gets a prison sentence," because "his wife will reward him" or because "the pharmacist was not prepared to do an honest deal. He mistreated Heinz, so Heinz is justified in doing the same in return." Alternatively Heinz should not steal the medicine because "prison is a horrible place and he will endure worse suffering there than if his wife dies."

At stages 3 and 4, associated with the conventional level, people take into account the conventions, values, norms, and expectations of their environment. Stage 3 is the phase of "interpersonal accord" and conformity: it is important to be a good person by being helpful to people around you. Mutual loyalty, trust, and friendship determine morality. Arguments for stealing are, for example, "Heinz loves his wife and wants to save her," "his wife expects this of him," and "no man can stand by and watch passively as his wife dies." Arguments against stealing are, for example, that "stealing is wrong and Heinz would not want to be a criminal" and "Heinz has done everything he could without breaking the law."

Stage 4 is the level at which people are guided by social order and authority in determining right and wrong. Rules and social etiquette are recognized as necessary for the functioning of society. Anyone who resists this endangers society and thereby does wrong. The need for agreement from others, present at stage 3, disappears, since people are now subordinate to society. Viewpoints held at stage 4 are, for instance, "Heinz should not steal the medicine because the law prohibits theft and this makes it illegal" and "Heinz should not steal the medicine because if everyone did this then society would be chaos," or "Heinz should steal the medicine but also serve his prison sentence and pay the pharmacist what he is rightfully owed."

At the postconventional level people are less focused on maintaining society as it is, and more on the principles and values which make a *good* society. In stage 5, the stage of social contract and individual rights, society is seen as a social contract in which people participate and which serves everyone's interests. Of course there are different interests and values, but at the same time there are basic rights, such as freedom and life, which should be protected. Democratic procedures are important for improving society. People at this stage state that "Heinz should steal the medicine because everyone has a right to life, regardless of the law," or that "Heinz should not steal the medicine because the pharmacist has a right to fair compensation."

Stage 6, the final stage, is based on abstract reasoning about universal ethical principles. Morality is seen as an absolute principle. Whereas at stage 5 importance was still attached to democratic procedures, here it is a matter of universal perspective. Even in a democracy it is possible to make the wrong choices. Impartial and unbiased justice is therefore essential, allowing us to take an independent view of what is right and wrong. Characteristic of stage 6 are statements such as "Heinz should steal the medicine because saving a human life is of more fundamental value than the personal property rights of another person," or "Heinz should not steal the medicine because others need it just as much and their lives are as important as that of Heinz's wife."

Kohlberg defined the six stages and noted that people always progress through them in the same order, from 1 to 6. According to Kohlberg, the higher the better. However, people can get stuck at any level.

Kohlberg's model can be used in many different ways. You might use it to probe your own and your colleagues' level of argumentation. Like Kohlberg, you can present dilemmas to others and ask them for a reaction.

This not only tells you what kind of person you're dealing with, it may also help you to convince others. People's level indicates the type of argumentation they are most likely to be persuaded by. A person who thinks from the perspective of punishment will be more influenced by possible sanctions than someone who thinks from a group perspective.

This model offers some guidance as to the internal organization of a company. If personnel are at the preconventional level, a policy of sanctions should go down well. If they are at the conventional level, then it is important to set clear rules and make use of social control. In organizations in which the personnel are at the postconventional level, opening up a dialogue and exchanging points of view can be effective in coming to better founded principles. If people in an organization are at different levels, a custom solution will be needed.

Different studies have shown that people argue at a lower level when discussing work-related dilemmas than when they address private dilemmas. Simply giving them the Heinz dilemma is not sufficient to get a good view of the moral level within the organization. So if you would like to assess your own moral development or that of others, you would be best advised to use current, work-related dilemmas.

Challenge!

We have reached the end of the book. We have reviewed seven factors which explain the complex workings of right and wrong in the workplace. One of the recurrent themes was that people are susceptible to influences from their environment. This in itself is no bad thing, as long as we are aware of it and remain alert to bad influences. We can do this by questioning and confronting ourselves, by holding issues up to the light and cross-examining one another, in other words, by challenging. I will conclude by saying something more about this.

Challenge is a matter of confronting important issues in an open, constructive, stimulating manner, in order to open our eyes and ears and those of others. Challenge is about issues which matter to people, at the heart of which are values, norms, and interests. These are issues of right and wrong, responsibility and irresponsibility, moral and immoral.

Challenge occurs openly. People should not mince their words but should speak from the heart. This openness is constructive, because it is directed towards people gaining an improved understanding of one another, learning together and guarding against mistakes and transgressions. Challenge is not a matter of talking ourselves down into the dumps, wearing away at one another, putting one another down, or gossiping. This does not mean that constructive openness cannot be confrontational. Of course it can. Challenge is stimulating, in the sense that it confronts people, draws them out, attempts to get them thinking, and bring them to an understanding. It is a matter of addressing assumptions, viewpoints and ways of doing things, contesting them and raising questions without imposing an answer or starting out with a preconceived idea of the conclusion. Challenge is not pretentious. It does not suggest that one person has a monopoly on the truth, or is teaching the other a lesson and demanding that the other conform.

Challenge can begin with posing a question, expressing a feeling, or presenting an interesting example or dilemma. An introductory remark or stimulus of this kind is a challenge. Challenges come in all shapes and sizes.

They can be simple requests for further explanation, such as, "Aren't you jumping to conclusions?" or "Aren't we missing the point here?" They can also be questions which suggest a different way of looking at things, such as "How about looking at this from another point of view?" or "Where will we be in three years' time?" A challenge can be a question leading to a deeper level of communication, such as "What's your gut feeling?" and "Can we reconcile this with our starting point?" But a challenge can also be an expression of one's own emotions, such as "I feel uneasy about this" or "This is a step too far for me."

A challenge is a moment of intervention: a signal to stop what we're doing, call a time-out, and ask if we are doing the right thing, whether we have forgotten anything, whether we are listening to what others say and what we should be telling ourselves. When someone at work calls "challenge" or just "chall," it is a signal that he wants people to stop and focus on a particular issue.

Challenging issues enables organizations to self-cleanse and self-regulate. A couple of minutes' challenge can take place anywhere, in meetings, over coffee, in the workshop or at the counter. Alternatively, you could take it out into the fresh air. "Challenge sessions" provide an excellent opportunity to examine one another's behavior critically, tell the truth and listen to what both insiders and outsiders have to say, to look for wake-up calls and eye-openers.

In Chapter 52 we saw that according to Lawrence Kohlberg a person's moral level can be discerned from the arguments he uses in an ethical dilemma. This assumes that people present an argument. This is why an organization's moral level is reflected in the extent to which there is room for argumentation. Are people capable of challenging themselves and one another? Are they invited to do so? Are people who set a challenge heard, and questioned as to what they are saying? Are they valued and praised? And is this properly received?

In short, challenging oneself and one another is a powerful medicine against bad behavior. In fact, it is a powerful vitamin for a healthy organization and a healthy individual career.

Notes

Introduction

The quote by Jeffrey Skilling is taken from an article by Alexandre di Miceli da Silveira published on the website of the Social Science Research Network under the title "Corporate scandals of the earlier 21st century: Have we learned the lessons?"

I first presented the model of factors explaining unethical behavior in organizations in 1998 in my doctoral dissertation *Ethics management: Auditing and developing the ethical content of organizations* (Dordrecht: Springer). My most recent empirical study on the subject appeared in 2011 in the journal *Human Relations* under the title "Understanding unethical behavior by unraveling ethical culture." In this model role-modeling splits into top management role-modeling and supervisor role-modeling. For the sake of simplicity this distinction is not made in this book. The original model also makes a distinction between the factors of openness to discussion of dilemmas (discussability) and of confrontation of suspected unacceptable behavior (approachability). Since relatively little relevant experimental research has been carried out on confrontation, this factor is addressed together with openness.

1. Good or Bad by Nature? Empathy and Sympathy

For research into the moral evaluation of babies, see J. K. Hamlin, K. Wynn, and P. Bloom (2007), "Social evaluation by preverbal infants," *Nature*, 450: pp. 557–560. When the researchers used a figure with no eyes, the babies' preference disappeared altogether, because they no longer saw the game as social interaction.

Barack Obama's claim that greed caused the financial crisis comes from a speech on January 9, 2009. See www.upi.com/Top_News/2009/01/08/ Obama-Greed-led-to-economic-crisis/UPI-39941231434123/.

The term white-collar crime was coined by Edwin Sutherland. In his 1949 book *White Collar Crime* (New York: Dryden Press) he defines this as "crime committed by a person of respectability and high social status in the course of his occupation." He stated that white-collar criminals had different characteristics and motives from those of typical street criminals.

A classic article on the difference between an integrity approach and a compliance approach was written in 1994 by Linda Sharp Paine, under the title "Managing for organizational integrity," *Harvard Business Review*, 72(2): pp. 106–117.

2. What is My Price? Integrity as Supply and Demand

Michael Lewis's study on children telling lies is described in M. Lewis and C. Saarni (1993), *Lying and Deception in Everyday Life* (New York: Guilford Press).

3. Bagels at Work: Honesty and Dishonesty

The story of the bagel man is described in S. J. Dubner and S. D. Levitt (2004), "What the bagel man saw: An accidental glimpse at human nature" (*The New York Times Magazine*, June 6). It also appears in S. D. Levitt and S. J. Dubner (2005), *Freakonomics: A Rogue Economist Explores the Hidden Side of Everything* (New York: William Morrow).

For the study by Gabor and colleagues on overpaying and not waiting for change, see T. Gabor, J. Strean, G. Singh, and D. Varis (1986), "Public deviance: An experimental study," *Canadian Journal of Criminology*, 28: pp. 17–29. For the supporting study on returning change, see F. E. Rabinowitz, G. Colmar, D. Elgie, D. Hale, S. Niss, B, Sharp, and J. Singlitico (1993), "Dishonesty, indifference, or carelessness in souvenir shop transactions," *Journal of Social Psychology*, 133: pp. 73–79.

For the study on passengers who received too much change from bus drivers, see E. Yuchtman-Yaar and G. Rahav (1986), "Resisting small temptations in everyday transactions," *Journal of Social Psychology*, 126: pp. 23–30. Such studies are an effective way of testing people's honesty. Richard Wiseman researched honesty by offering to send people an exchange voucher for something they had not bought. Fifty percent of car dealers and priests responded and exchanged their vouchers. See R. Wiseman (2007), *Quirkology* (London: Pan Macmillan). Recent experimental research toward receiving excessive change has been conducted by Azar and colleagues finding that a majority of customers in a restaurant did not return the excessive change. Repeated customers returned the excessive change much more often than one-time customers and women returned the extra change much more often than men. See O. H. Azar, S. Yosef, and M. Bar-Eli (2013), "Do customers return excessive change in a restaurant? A field experiment on dishonesty," *Journal of Economic Behavior & Organization*, accepted but unpublished.

KPMG research on transgressions observed by employees in the workplace is published in M. Kaptein (2010), "The ethics of organizations: A longitudinal study of the U.S. working population," *Journal of Business Ethics*, 92: pp. 601−618. Most recent KPMG research of the U.S. working population has been conducted in 2013.

4. Egoism versus Altruism: The Theory of the Warm Glow and the Helping Hand

Research showing that people are made happier by helping was carried out by, among others, E. Dunn, L. Aknin, and M. Norton (2008), "Spending money on others promotes happiness," *Science*, 319: pp. 1687−1688. See also S. Lyubomisky, K. M. Sheldon, and D. Schkade (2005), "Pursuing happiness: The architecture of sustainable change," *Review of General Psychology*, 9: pp. 111−131.

Research on altruism in young children was carried out by F. Warneken and M. Tomasello (2006), "Altruistic helping in human infants and young chimpanzees," *Science*, 311: pp. 1301−1303.

Daniel Batson collaborated with colleagues to carry out a great deal of research into the situations in which people are altruistic. One of his latest articles is C. D. Batson, J. H. Eklund, V. L. Chermok, J. L. Hoyt, and B. G. Ortiz (2007), "An additional antecedent of empathic concern: Valuing the welfare of the person in need," *Journal of Personality and Social Psychology*, 93: pp. 65−74.

5. What You Expect Is What You Get: the Pygmalion and Golem Effects

The research on the Pygmalion effect in the American elementary school is described in R. Rosenthal and L. F. Jacobson (1968), *Pygmalion in the Classroom: Teacher Expectation and Pupils' Intellectual Development* (New York: Holt). The research has been repeated several times with approximately the same results. See R. Rosenthal (1994), "Interpersonal expectancy effects: A 30-year perspective," *Current Directions in Psychological*

Science, 3: pp. 176–179. Meta-analyses on the Pygmalion effect in organizations have been carried out by Nicole Kierein and Michael Gold as well as Brian McNatt. They conclude that this is a significant effect. See N. M. Kierein and M. A. Gold (2000), "Pygmalion in work organizations: A meta-analysis," *Journal of Organizational Behavior*, 21: pp. 913–928, and D. B. McNatt (2000), "Ancient Pygmalion joins contemporary management: A meta-analysis of the result," *Journal of Applied Psychology*, 85: pp. 314–322.

Research has also been carried out into the Pygmalion effect in love. In their experiment Mark Snyder and colleagues had men call a woman they did not know. The men received a photo of a woman, which in reality was randomly selected. The more beautiful the woman in the photo, the more warmly the men spoke, with the result that the woman spoke warmly in response, confirming the men in the idea that the woman must be beautiful. See M. Snyder, E. Decker Tanke, and E. Berscheid (1977), "Social perception and interpersonal behavior: On the self-fulfilling nature of social stereotypes," *Journal of Personality and Social Psychology*, 35: pp. 655–666.

6. Self-Image and Behavior: The Galatea Effect

For the research into the influence of free will on cheating, see K. D. Vohs and J. W. Schooler (2008), "The value of believing in free will: Encouraging a belief in determinism increases cheating," *Psychological Science*, 19: pp. 49–54.

The Galatea effect was introduced by Robert Merton in 1957 in his book *Social Theory and Social Structure* (New York: Free Press).

Talking more quietly when thinking of a library is an effect demonstrated by Henk Aarts and Ap Dijksterhuis. See their article published in 2003, "The silence of the library: Environment, situational norm, and social behavior," *Journal of Personality and Social Psychology*, 84: pp. 18–28.

7. Self-Knowledge and Mirages: Self-Serving Biases and the Dodo Effect

For the better-than-average effect see M. D. Alicke, M. L. KLotz, D. L. Breitenbecher, T. J. Yurak, and D. S. Vredenburg (1995), "Personal contact, individuation, and the better-than-average effect," *Journal of Personality and Social Psychology*, 68: pp. 804–825. The study on couples sharing household chores was carried out by Michael Ross and Firore

Sicoly and published in 1982 as "Egocentric biases in availability and attribution," in D. Kahneman, P. Slovic, and A. Tversky (Eds.), *Judgment under Uncertainty: Heuristics and Biases* (Cambridge: Cambridge University Press): pp. 179—189.

A good article on biases and the ethical risks attached to them is M. Banaji, M. Bazerman, and D. Chug (2003), "How (un)ethical are you?" *Harvard Business Review*, December: pp. 56—64.

The fact that 90 percent of managers in the United States consider themselves to be functioning above average is described in P. Zimbardo (2007), *The Lucifer Effect: Understanding How Good People Turn Evil* (New York: Random House).

The phenomenon of ethical mirages is described in A. E. Tenbrunsel, K. A. Diekmann, K. A. Wade-Benzoni, and M. H. Bazerman (2010), "The Ethical Mirage: A temporal explanation as to why we are not as ethical as we think we are," *Research in Organizational Behavior*, 30: pp. 153—173.

The research on the value of unpacking is published as E. Caruso, N. Epley, and M. Bazerman (2006), "The costs and benefits of undoing egocentric responsibility assessments," *Journal of Personality and Social Psychology*, 91(5): pp. 857—871.

8. Apples, Barrels, and Orchards: Dispositional, Situational, and Systemic Causes

For the study on parking offences by diplomats, see R. Fisman and E. Miguel (2007), "Corruption, norms, and legal enforcement: Evidence from diplomatic parking tickets," *Journal of Political Economy*, 115: pp. 1020—1048.

The studies by Abigail Barr and Danila Serra cited are published as A. Barr and D. Serra (2006), "Culture and corruption," *University of Oxford research paper*, and A. Barr and D. Serra (2008), "Culture and corruption: An experimental analysis," *University of Oxford research paper*.

The statement that "It is sometimes less difficult for a new police officer to become corrupt than to remain honest" was made by Whiteman Knapp in 1973 as chair of the Knapp Commission for research into police corruption. See The Knapp Commission (1973), *Report on Police Corruption* (New York: G. Braziller).

9. Flyers and Norms: Cognitive Stimuli

The research by Cialdini on flyers appeared in R. B. Cialdini, R. R. Reno, and C. A. Kallgren (1990), "A focus theory of normative conduct:

Recycling the concept of norms to reduce littering in public places," *Journal of Personality and Social Psychology*, 58: pp. 1015–1026. Cialdini has carried out extensive research on how the influence works. See his book, first published in 1984, and appearing in its 5th revised edition in 2009, *Influence: Science and Practice* (Boston: Pearson Education). See also N. J. Goldstein, S. J. Martin, and R. B. Cialdini (2007), *Yes!: 50 Scientifically Proven Ways to be Persuasive* (New York: Free Press).

10. The Ten Commandments and Fraud: Affective Stimuli

The research into the relationship between the Ten Commandments and Fraud was described in N. Mazar, O. Amir, and D. Ariely (2008), "The dishonesty of honest people: A theory of self-concept maintenance," *Journal of Marketing Research*, XL: pp. 633–644.

The study on the relationship between the nonexistent code of conduct and fraudulent behavior was carried out by N. Mazar and D. Ariely (2006), "Dishonesty in everyday life and its policy implications," *Journal of Public Policy and Marketing*, 25: pp. 1–21.

Research of Lisa Shu and colleagues shows that giving a nudge at the right moment can make a big difference. Using laboratory and field experiments, they found that signing written forms before rather than after the opportunity to cheat significantly reduces dishonest self-reports. See L. L. Shu, N. Mazar, F. Gino, D. Ariely, and M. H. Bazerman (2012), "Signing at the beginning makes ethics salient and decreases dishonest self-reports in comparison to signing at the end," *Proceedings of the National Academy of Sciences of the United States of America*, 109: pp. 15197–15200.

A book worth reading on the use of checklists is Atul Gawande's (2009), *The Checklist Manifesto: How to Get Things Right* (New York: Metropolitan Books). For an explanation of the way in which little nudges can stimulate people's notion of norms, see R. H. Thaler and C. R. Sunstein (2008), *Nudge: Improving Decisions about Health, Wealth, and Happiness*, (New Haven: Yale University Press).

11. The Name of the Game: Euphemisms and Spoilsports

The American National Sleep Foundation regularly publishes research on the relationship between work and sleep. See www.sleepfoundation.org.

Albert Bandura has published a great deal on euphemisms. For example, see A. Bandura (1999), "Moral disengagement in the perpetration of inhumanities," *Personality and Social Psychology Review*, 3: pp. 193–209.

For the study on the difference between playing the "Wall Street Game" and the "Community Game" on participants' behavior, see V. Liberman, S. M. Samuels, and L. Ross (2004), "The name of the game: Predictive power of reputations versus situational labels in determining prisoner's dilemma game moves," *Personality and Social Psychology Bulletin*, 30: pp. 1175–1185.

An interesting article claiming that business is not a game is Maurice Hamington's paper published in 2009, "Business is not a game: The metaphoric fallacy," *Journal of Business Ethics*, 86: pp. 473–484.

12. Hypegiaphobia: The Fear Factor of Rules

On the relationship between rules and incidents in hospitals see T. Katz-Navon, E. Naveh, and Z. Stern (2005), "Safety climate in health care organizations: A multidimensional approach," *Academy of Management Journal*, 48(6): pp. 1075–1089.

13. Rules Create Offenders and Forbidden Fruits Taste the Best: Reactance Theory

For the study on graffiti on the wall and its relationship to prohibitions, see J. Pennebaker and D. Sanders (1976), "American graffiti: Effects of authority and reactance arousal," *Personality and Social Psychology Bulletin*, 2: pp. 264–267.

Publications describing reactance theory include T. Hammock and J. W. Brehm (1966), "The attractiveness of choice alternatives when freedom to choose is eliminated by a social agent," *Journal of Personality*, 34: pp. 546–554.

For the effects of smoking bans on behavior, see J. Grandpre, E. M. Alvaro, M. Burgoon, C. H. Miller, and J. R. Hall (2003), "Adolescent reactance and anti-smoking campaigns: A theoretical approach," *Health Communication*, 15(3): pp. 349–366. A related article is H. Miller, L. T. Lane, L. M. Deatrick, A. M. Young, and K. A. Potts (2007), "Psychological reactance and promotional health messages: The effects of controlling language," *Human Communication Research*, 33: pp. 219–240.

For the research into the attractiveness of unobtainable objects, see S. S. Brehm (1981), "Psychological reactance and the attractiveness of unobtainable objects: Sex differences in children's responses to an elimination of freedom," *Sex Roles*, 7: pp. 937–949.

14. What Happens Normally Is the Norm: Descriptive and Injunctive Norms

The research by Cialdini on flyers appeared in R. B. Cialdini, R. R. Reno, and C. A. Kallgren (1990), "A focus theory of normative conduct: Recycling the concept of norms to reduce littering in public places," *Journal of Personality and Social Psychology*, 58: pp. 1015–1026. Other publications by these researchers in the same area include C. A. Kallgren, R. R. Reno, and R. B. Cialdini (2003), "A focus theory of normative conduct: When norms do and do not affect behavior," *Personality and Social Psychology Bulletin*, 26: pp. 1002–1012; R. B. Cialdini (2003), "Crafting normative messages to protect the environment," *Current Directions in Psychological Science*, 12: pp. 105–109; R. B. Cialdini, L. J. Demaine, B. J. Sagarin, D. W. Barret, K. Rhoads, and P. L. Winter (2006), "Managing social norms for persuasive impact," *Social Influence*, 1: pp. 3–15.

The experiment by K. Keizer is described in *The spreading of disorder*, University of Groningen, 2010, and in K. Keizer, S. Lindenberg, and L. Steg (2008), "The spreading of disorder," *Science*, 322: pp. 1681–1685.

Much research has been conducted into mirroring behavior. Tania Singer and colleagues demonstrated that when one member of a couple is in pain, the same parts of the on-looking partner's brain are activated, at least in those cases in which there is real affection in the relationship. See T. Singer, B. Seymour, J. O'Doherty, H. Kaube, R. J. Dolan, and C. D. Frith (2004), "Empathy for pain involves the affective but not sensory components of pain," *Science*, 303: pp. 1157–1162.

15. Broken Panes Bring Bad Luck: The Broken Window Theory

For the broken window theory, see J. Wilson and G. L. Kelling (1982), "Broken windows: The police and neighborhood safety," *The Atlantic Monthly*, 249: pp. 29–38.

The experiment by Kees Keizer is described in *The spreading of disorder*, University of Groningen, 2010, and in K. Keizer, S. Lindenberg, and L. Steg (2008), "The spreading of disorder," *Science*, 322: pp. 1681–1685. In Freakonomics (2005), Steven Levitt and Stephen Dubner discuss arguments for and against the idea that the broken window theory was the cause of the reduction in crime in New York.

16. The Office as a Reflection of the Inner Self: Interior Decoration and Architecture

For the study suggesting that weapons arouse aggression, see L. Berkowitz and A. LePage (1967), "Weapons as aggression-eliciting stimuli," *Journal of Personality and Social Psychology*, 7: pp. 202–207.

For Andrew Lohmann and colleagues' research claiming that the decoration of the living room reflects the quality of the residents' relationship, see A. Lohmann, A. B. Arriaga, and W. Goodfriend (2003), "Close relationships and placemaking: Do objects in a couple's home reflect couplehood?" *Personal Relationships*, 10: pp. 437–450.

17. The Need for Ethical Leadership: Moral Compass and Courage

Much research has been conducted on the influence of good examples. James Bryan and Mary Test, as well as Jacqueline Macaulay and Leonard Berkowitz, show that when one person gives money to a busker, others are more likely to do the same. See J. H. Bryan and M. A. Test (1967), "Models and helping: Naturalistic studies in aiding behavior," *Journal of Personality and Social Psychology*, 6: pp. 400–407; J. Macaulay and L. Berkowitz (1970), *Altruism and Helping Behavior* (New York: Academic Press).

Social learning theory is described in A. Bandura (1997), *Social Learning Theory* (Englewood Cliffs: Prentice Hall).

Kees Keizer's experiments on the influence of role models is described in his doctoral dissertation *The spreading of disorder*, University of Groningen, 2010. Susan Andersen and Steve Cole observed that information about significant others is more richly connected in the brain and can be more easily accessed than information about insignificant others. See S. M. Andersen and S. W. Cole (1990), "'Do I Know You?': The role of significant others in general social perception," *Journal of Personality and Social Psychology*, 59: pp. 384–399.

For press coverage of the boss who made herself redundant, see P. Thompson (2010), "Woman hailed as best boss in America after firing herself to spare the jobs of her staff" (*Mail Online*, November 29, 2010).

18. Morals Melt under Pressure: Authority and Obedience

For the study involving inappropriate requests to nurses, see C. K. Hofling, E. Brotzman, S. Dalrymple, N. Graves, and C. M. Pierce (1966),

"An experimental study in nurse-physician relationships," *Journal of Nervous and Mental Disease*, 143: pp. 171–180.

Milgram's study is described in S. Milgram (1963), "Behavioral study of obedience," *Journal of Abnormal and Social Psychology*, 67: pp. 371–378 and in S. Milgram (1974), *Obedience to Authority: An Experimental View* (New York: HarperCollins).

For an overview of other studies with similar findings to Milgram's, see T. Blass (1999), "The Milgram paradigm after 35 years: Some things we now know about obedience to authority," *Journal of Applied Social Psychology*, 29: pp. 955–978. To exclude the possibility that the participants suspected actors were involved, a follow-up study was conducted, this time inflicting real shocks on dogs in full view of the subjects. The participants saw the dogs being electrocuted, but this did nothing to change their obedience. Fifty percent of the men and 100 percent of the women administered the maximum shock. See C. L. Sheridan and R. G. King (1972), "Obedience to authority with an authentic victim," *Proceedings of the eightieth annual convention of the American Psychological Association* (Washington: American Psychological Association): pp. 165–166.

19. Trapped in the Role: Clothes Make the Man

For the study on power dressing see S. Tzioti (2010), *Let me give you a piece of advice: Empirical papers about advice taking in marketing*, Doctoral dissertation (Rotterdam: Erasmus Research Institute of Management).

The study by Dan Ariely on provocative clothing was described in his 2008 book, *Predictably Irrational: The Hidden Forces that Shape Our Decisions* (New York: HarperCollins). Leonard Bickman conducted experimental research demonstrating the social power of uniforms. See L. Bickman (1974), "The social power of a uniform," *Journal of Applied Social Psychology*, 4: pp. 47–61.

The Stanford Prison Experiment is described in P. Zimbardo (2007), *The Lucifer Effect: Understanding How Good People Turn Evil* (New York: Random House). Scott Fraser's study on the relationship between clothing and choice of games has never been published. The study is cited in the above-mentioned book by Philip Zimbardo.

20. Power Corrupts, But Not Always: Hypocrisy and Hypercrisy

The research on hypocrisy is described in J. Lammers, D. A. Stapel, and A. D. Galinsky (2010), "Power increases hypocrisy: Moralizing in reasoning, immorality in behavior," *Psychological Science*, 21: pp. 737–744. Another study shows that powerful people think more in terms of the rules (deontologically), whereas less powerful people think more in terms of results (teleologically). See J. Lammers and D. Stapel (2009), "How power influences moral thinking," *Journal of Personality and Social Psychology*, 97: pp. 279–289.

For another publication on leaders' sense of entitlement, see D. de Cremer, E. van Dijk, and C. P. Reinders Folmer (2009), "Why leaders feel entitled to take more: Feelings of entitlement as a moral rationalization strategy" in D. de Cremer (Ed.), *Psychological Perspectives on Ethical Behavior and Decision Making* (Charlotte: Information Age Publishing): pp. 107–119.

21. Beeping Bosses: Fear, Aggression, and Uncertainty

The study on beeping cars can be found in A. Diekman, M. Jungbauer-Gans, H. Krassnig, and S. Lorenz (1996), "Social status and aggression: A field study analyzed by survival analysis," *Journal of Social Psychology*, 136: pp. 761–768.

Bernie Ebbers is mentioned in David R. Lease (2006), "From great to ghastly: How toxic organizational cultures poison companies," Paper presentation at the Academy of Business Education. Dick Fuld's description is taken from the BBC documentary on the fall of Lehman Brothers, entitled "The Love of Money."

For Nathanael Fast and Serena Chen's research on how people in leadership positions respond to feelings of uncertainty, see N. J. Fast and S. Chen (2009), "When the boss feels inadequate: Power, incompetence, and aggression," *Psychological Science*, 20: pp. 1406–1413.

22. Fare Dodgers and Black Sheep: When Model Behavior Backfires

For the study on dog owners cleaning up after their pets, see P. Webley and C. Siviter (2000), "Why do some owners allow their dogs to foul the pavement? The social psychology of a minor rule infraction," *Journal of Applied Social Psychology*, 30: pp. 1371–1380. A similar effect is shown in research by G. C. Thomas, C. D. Batson, and J. S. Coke (1981), "Do good Samaritans discourage helpfulness? Self-perceived altruism after exposure to highly helpful others," *Journal of Personality and Social Psychology*, 40: pp. 194–200. This research shows that when people are exposed to very helpful people they see themselves as less altruistic and are therefore less willing to help others than people who are exposed to someone of average helpfulness. The first group see themselves as less intrinsically motivated because they are less able to choose for themselves, with the result that they help less. This is an undesirable side effect of role-modeling.

For Francesca Gino and colleagues' research into the way in which a rotten apple contaminates the rest of the barrel, see F. Gino, S. Ayal, and D. Ariely (2009), "Contagion and differentiation in unethical behavior: The effect of one bad apple on the barrel," *Psychological Science*, 20: pp. 393–398. In a similar experiment, Robert Cialdini and colleagues varied the number of pieces of rubbish in the area. 358 amusement park visitors were given a flyer with the text "Don't miss tonight's show." The visitors were approached just before they walked around a corner, taking them out of sight of the person handing out the flyers. The visitors now found themselves on a path roughly 55 meters long. There were no paths leading off it, nor were there any trash cans. The more flyers on the ground, the more the visitors threw their flyers on the ground too. When there were no flyers on the ground, 18 percent of the visitors threw theirs away; with two and four flyers on the ground respectively, 20 percent and 23 percent were thrown away; and with eight on the ground, 41 percent were thrown away. The percentage did not rise when more than eight flyers were on the ground. But what happened when there was just 1 flyer on the ground? Only 10 percent of visitors threw away their flyers, the lowest figure across all scenarios. It also turned out that the more flyers on the ground, the quicker visitors threw theirs away, but when only one flyer was on the ground, the visitors were slowest to throw theirs away. See B. Cialdini, R. R. Reno, and C. A. Kallgren (1990), "A focus theory of normative conduct: Recycling the concept of norms to reduce littering in public places," *Journal of Personality and Social Psychology*, 58(6): pp. 1015–1026.

Philip Tetlock and colleagues show that even reading about reprehensible behavior by others encourages sociable behavior. The participants in their experiment who read about someone who supported bad behavior felt morally contaminated and were more inclined to participate in volunteer work for a campaign against this behavior than the participants who had not read this material. See P. E. Tetlock, O. Kristel, B. Elson, M. Green, and J. Lerner (2000), "The psychology of the unthinkable: Taboo trade-offs, forbidden base rates, and heretical counterfactuals," *Journal of Personality and Social Psychology*, 78: pp. 853–870.

More on the black-sheep effect can be read in A. C. Lewis and S. J. Sherman (2010), "Perceived entitativity and the black-sheep effect: When will we denigrate negative ingroup members?" *Journal of Social Psychology*, 150(2): pp. 211–225.

23. Goals and Blinkers: Tunnel Vision and Teleopathy

The parable of the Sadhu is described in B. H. McCoy (1983), "The parable of the Sadhu," *Harvard Business Review*, September/October: pp. 103–108.

For Barry Staw and Richard Boettger's research on how focusing on a goal can lead to other things being ignored, see B. M. Staw and R. D. Boettger (1990), "Task revision: A neglected form of work performance," *Academy of Management Journal*, 33: pp. 534–559.

For Daniel Simons and Christopher Chabris' experiment on seeing the gorilla, see D. J. Simons and C. F. Chabris (1999), "Gorillas in our midst: Sustained inattentional blindness for dynamic events," *Perception*, 28: pp. 1059–1074.

Research by James Shah and colleagues shows that when confronted with multiple goals, people tend to focus on one. See J. Y. Shah, R. Friedman, and A. W. Kruglanski (2002), "Forgetting all else: On the antecedents and consequences of goal shielding," *Journal of Personality and Social Psychology*, 83: pp. 1261–1280.

Another study shows that when people have both qualitatively and quantitatively challenging goals, they sacrifice the qualitative goals in favor of the quantitative goals. Goals which can more easily be attained and measured, such as quantity, receive more attention in a multiple goal scenario. See S. W. Gilliland and R. S. Landis (1992), "Quality and quantity goals in a complex decision task: Strategies and outcomes," *Journal of Applied Psychology*, 77: pp. 672–681.

24. Own Goals: Seeing Goals as the Ceiling

For the study on taxi drivers in New York, see C. Camerer, L. Babcock, G. Loewenstein, and R. Thaler (1997), "Labor supply of New York City cabdrivers: One day at a time," *The Quarterly Journal of Economics*, 112(2): pp. 407–441.

The theory of "perceived behavioral control" is described in work by Icek Ajzen among others. See I. Ajzen (2002), "Perceived behavioral control, self-efficacy, locus of control, and the theory of planned behavior," *Journal of Applied Social Psychology*, 32: pp. 665–683. See also I. Ajzen and M. Fishbein (1980), *Understanding Attitudes and Predicting Social Behavior* (Englewood-Cliffs: Prentice Hall).

Research by Richard Larrick and colleagues into how specific and challenging goals lead to more risky behavior can be found in R. P. Larrick, C. Heath, and G. Wu (2009), "Goal-induced risk taking in negotiation and decision making," *Social Cognition*, 27: pp. 342–364.

The goal ladder, as described by Minjung Koo and Ayelet Fishbach, appeared in M. Koo and A. Fishbach (2010), "Climbing the goal ladder: How upcoming actions increase level of aspiration," *Journal of Personality and Social Psychology*, 99: pp. 1–13. Their research shows that when people are more focused on actions still to be completed, as opposed to goals they have already achieved, this encourages them to climb further up the ladder.

25. The Winner Takes it All: Losing Your Way in the Maze of Competition

For the research by Christiane Schwieren and Doris Weichselbaumer into the extent to which competition encourages cheating, see C. Schwieren and D. Weichselbaumer (2010), "Does competition enhance performance or cheating?" *Journal of Economic Psychology*, 31: pp. 241–253.

For the study by Maurice Schweitzer and colleagues showing that people who are just short of their goal are most inclined to cheat, see M. E. Schweitzer, L. Ordonez, and B. Douma (2004), "Goal setting as a motivator of unethical behavior," *Academy of Management Journal*, 47: pp. 422–432.

26. From Jerusalem to Jericho: Time Pressure and Slack

For the study on theology students under pressure, see J. M. Darley and C. D. Batson (1973), "From Jerusalem to Jericho: A study of situational variables in helping behavior," *Journal of Personality and Social Psychology*, 27: pp. 100–108. See also C. D. Batson, P. J. Cochran, M. F. Biederman, and J. L. Bloser (1978), "Failure to help in a hurry: Callousness or conflict," *Personality and Social Psychology Bulletin*, 4: pp. 97–101.

Philip Zimbardo also shows in his prison experiment (Chapter 19) that the lack of a sense of time promotes reprehensible behavior. The participants in the prison had no sense of the time and behaved badly for the sake of killing time.

27. Moral Muscle: The Importance of Sleep and Sugar

For the research showing that tiredness leads to reduced self-control and more cheating, see N. L. Mead, R. F. Baumeister, F. Gino, M. E. Schweitzer, and D. Ariely (2009), "Too tired to tell the truth: Self-control resource depletion and dishonesty," *Journal of Experimental Social Psychology*, 45: pp. 594–597.

Various experiments by Mark Muraven and Roy Baumeister show that self-control is sapped when it is frequently put to the test. See, for example, M. Muraven, D. M. Tice, and R. F. Baumeister (1998), "Self-control as limited resource: Regulatory depletion patterns," *Journal of Personality and Social Psychology*, 74(3): pp. 774–789; M. Muraven and E. Slessareva (2003), "Mechanisms of self-control failure: Motivation and limited resources," *Personality and Social Psychology Bulletin*, 29(7): pp. 894–906; R. F. Baumeister, E. Bratslavsky, M. Muraven, and D. M. Tice (1998), "Ego-depletion: Is the active self a limited resource?" *Journal of Personality and Social Psychology*, 74: pp. 1252–1265; M. Muraven and R. F. Baumeister (2000), "Self-regulation and depletion of limited resources: Does self-control resemble a muscle?" *Psychological Bulletin*, 126: pp. 247–259.

For the study on the effect of sleep deprivation on moral judgment, see W. D. S. Killgore, D. B. Killgore, L. M. Day, C. Li, G. H. Kamimori, and T. J. Balkin (2007), "The effects of 53 hours of sleep deprivation on moral judgment," *Sleep*, 30: pp. 345–352.

Research by Matthew Gailliot and Roy Baumeister shows that activities requiring self-control lead to lower blood sugar levels. See M. T. Gailliot and R. F. Baumeister (2007), "The physiology of willpower: Linking blood glucose to self-control," *Personality and Social Psychology Review*, 11: pp. 303–327. In folllow-up research, subjects who drank lemonade sweetened with sugar had better self-control than subjects who drank artificially sweetened lemonade. See E. J. Masicampo and R. F. Baumeister (2008), "Toward a physiology of dual-process reasoning and judgment: Lemonade, willpower, and expensive rule-based analysis," *Psychological Science*, 19: pp. 255–260.

The effect of skipping breakfast is demonstrated by A. P. Smith, R. Clark, and J. Gallagher (1999), "Breakfast cereal and caffeinated coffee: Effects on working memory, attention, mood, and cardiovascular function," *Physiology and Behavior*, 67: pp. 9–17.

For an overview of research showing that criminals, fraudsters, vandals, and traffic offenders have low blood sugar, see M. T. Gailliot and R. F. Baumeister (2007), "The physiology of willpower: Linking blood glucose to self-control," *Personality and Social Psychology Review*, 11: pp. 303–327. Rojas and Sanchi, for example, found that approximately 90 percent of the offenders they studied had relatively low blood glucose (although the relationship may be reversed, with reduced blood glucose occurring as a result of the offense and arrest). See N. Rojas and A. F. Sanchi (1941), "Hipoglucemia en delincuentes," *Archivos Medicales Legal Identificacion*, 11: p. 29.

28. The Future under Control: Implementation Plans and Coffee Cups

For research into the power of implementation plans at a telecoms company see R. W. Holland, H. Aarts, and D. Langendam (2006), "Breaking and creating habits on the working floor: A field-experiment on the power of implementation intentions," *Journal of Experimental Social Psychology*, 42: pp. 776–783.

For the study on the effect of resolutions which fail to stipulate activities to be replaced, see B. Verplanken and S. Faes (1999), "Good intentions, bad habits, and effects of forming implementation intentions on healthy eating," *European Journal of Social Psychology*, 29: pp. 591–604.

On the power of a public commitment, see P. Sheeran and S. Orbell (1999), "Implementation intentions and repeated behaviour: Augmenting the predictive validity of the theory of planned behavior," *European Journal of Social Psychology*, 29: pp. 349–369.

For Danny Axsom and Joel Cooper's experiment involving women who wished to lose weight, see D. Axsom and J. Cooper (1985), "Cognitive dissonance and psychotherapy: The role of effort justification in inducing weight loss," *Journal of Experimental Social Psychology*, 21: pp. 149–160.

Incidentally, those who believe that the problem of recycling plastic cups can be solved simply by placing a recycle bin in every office are wrong. Holland and colleagues' research showed that this also failed, except when employees first came up with an implementation plan.

Francesca Gino explores in her book *Sidedtracked* (Boston: Harvard Business School Publishing, 2013) all kinds of factors that lead to inconsistent decisions people make.

29. Ethics on the Slide Leads to Slip-Ups: Escalating Commitment and the Induction Mechanism

The six phases of corruption are described in L. W. Sherman (1985), "Becoming bent: Moral careers of corrupt policemen," in F. A. Elliston and M. Feldberg (Eds.), *Moral Issues in Police Work* (Totowa: Rowman and Allanheld).

For Judson Mills's experiment at the elementary school see J. Mills (1958), "Changes in moral attitudes following temptation," *Journal of Personality*, 26: pp. 517–531.

30. The Foot-in-the-Door and Door-in-the-Face Techniques: Self-Perception Theory

The low-ball tactic is described in R. B. Cialdini, J. T. Cacioppo, R. Bassett, and J. A. Miller (1978), "Low-ball procedure for producing compliance; commitment then cost," *Journal of Personality and Social Psychology*, 36: pp. 463–476.

For the foot-in-the-door tactic, see J. L. Freedman and S. C. Fraser (1966), "Compliance without pressure: The foot-in-the-door technique," *Journal of Personality and Social Psychology*, 4: pp. 195–203. Follow-up research was conducted by M. Snyder and M. R. Cunningham (1975), "To comply or not comply: Testing the self-perception explanation of the 'foot-in-the-door' phenomenon," *Journal of Personality and Social Psychology*, 31: pp. 64–67, and M. Bush and K. Kirsch (1976), "Relationship between compliance in the foot-in-the-door paradigm and size of first request," *Journal of Personality and Social Psychology*, 33: pp. 517–520.

For the door-in-the-face tactic, see R. B. Cialdini, J. E. Vincent, S. K. Lewis, J. Catalan, D. Wheeler, and B. L. Darby (1975), "Reciprocal concessions procedure for inducing compliance: The door-in-the-face technique," *Journal of Personality and Social Psychology*, 31: pp. 206–215.

For an extensive description of tactics of persuasion, see R. B. Cialdini (2009), *Influence: Science and Practice* (Boston: Pearson Education, 5th edition).

For a description of the relative effectiveness of the persuasive tactics described in this chapter, see R. J. Brownstein and R. D. Kattzev (1985), "The relative effectiveness of three compliance techniques in eliciting donations to a cultural organization," *Journal of Applied Social Psychology*, 15: pp. 564–574.

31. So Long as the Music Is Playing: Sound Waves and Magnetic Waves

For research into the relationship between background music and purchasing behavior, see C. S. Areni and D. Kim (1993), "The influence of background music on shopping behavior: Classical versus top-forty music in a wine store," *Advances in Consumer Research*, 20: pp. 336–340. For research into the relationship between country music and suicide, see S. Stack and J. Gundlach (1992), "The effect of country music on suicide," *Social Forces*, 71: pp. 211–218.

For Liane Yong and colleagues' research on the influence of magnetic fields on moral judgment, see L. Young, J. Camprodon, M. Hauser, A. Pascual-Leone, and R. Saxe (2010), "Disruption of the right temporo-parietal junction with transcranial magnetic stimulation reduces the role of beliefs in moral judgment," *Proceedings of the National Academy of Sciences of the United States of America*, 107: pp. 6753–6758.

32. Feeling Good and Doing Good: Mood and Atmosphere

Much research has been conducted on the relationship between mood and decision-making. See, for example, A. M. Isen and R. Patrick (1983), "The effect of positive feelings on risk taking: When the chips are down," *Organizational Behavior and Human Performance*, 31: pp. 194–202; G. F. Loewenstein, E. U. Weber, C. K. Hsee, and N. Welch (2001), "Risk as feelings," *Psychological Bulletin*, 127(2): pp. 267–286. See also M. H. Bazerman and D. A. Moore (2009), *Judgment in Managerial Decision Making* (New York: Wiley, 7th edition).

For Nicolas Guéguen's study on jokes in a French bar, see N. Guéguen (2002), "The effects of a joke on tipping when it is delivered at the same time as the bill," *Journal of Applied Social Psychology*, 32: pp. 1955–1963.

For Nicolas Guéguen and Patrick Legoherel's research on the effect of drawing a happy face on the check on subsequent tips, see N. Guéguen and P. Legoherel (2000), "Effect on tipping of barman drawing a sun on the bottom of customers' check," *Psychological Reports*, 87: pp. 223–226. See also B. Rind and P. Bordia (1995), "Effect of servers' 'Thank You' and personalization on restaurant tipping," *Journal of Applied Social Psychology*, 25: pp. 745–751. The tip also rises significantly when the waiting staff introduce themselves by their first names or address the client by name, as described in K. Garrity and D. Degelman (1990), "Effect of server introduction on restaurant tipping," *Journal of Applied Social Psychology*, 20: pp. 168–172. Touching the client can also raise the tip, as shown in A. H. Crusco and C. G. Wetzel (1984), "The Midas touch: The effects of interpersonal touch on restaurant tipping," *Personality and Social Psychology Bulletin*, 10: pp. 512–517.

The principle of "feeling good and doing good" is also illustrated by Alice Isen and Paula Levin in: A. M. Isen and P. A. Levin (1972), "Effect of feeling good on helping: Cookies and kindness," *Journal of Personality and Social Psychology*, 21: pp. 384–388.

Research into the flipside of a good mood has been conducted by Georgina Craciun, as published in her doctoral dissertation, *Mood effects on ordinary unethical behavior* of 2006 at the University of South Carolina.

33. A Personal Face Social Bond Theory and Lost Property

Research showing that many employees would not recognize their organization's director was carried out, among others, by De Vos and Jansen in their 2010 study *Undercover Boss*.

The experiment with the lost and found purses was conducted and described by Richard Wiseman in 2009 in his book *59 Seconds: Think a Little, Change a Lot* (London: Macmillan).

Social bond theory was described by Travis Hirschi in 1969 in his book *Causes of Delinquency* (Berkeley: University of California Press).

Debora Small and George Loewenstein conducted research showing that a visible face generates more empathy and sympathy, in turn leading people to donate more to a victim with a face than to an unknown victim. See D. Small and G. Loewenstein (2003), "Helping *a* victim or helping *the* victim: Altruism and identifiability," *Journal of Risk and Uncertainty*, 26: pp. 5–16.

34. Cows and Post-It Notes: Love in the Workplace

For the research into the milk yield of cows, see C. Bertenshaw and P. Rowlinson (2009), "Exploring stock managers' perceptions of the human-animal relationship on dairy farms and an association with milk production," *Anthrozoös*, 22: pp. 59–69.

For the study by a national tax authority on the use of Post-it notes with handwritten text, see J. Croonen and L. Luesink (2009), *Met Andere Ogen: Het effect van verschillende beïnvloedingstechnieken op het aangiftegedrag van de ondernemer* (Seen through different eyes: The effect of different persuasive techniques on tax returns by businessmen), Dutch Tax and Customs Administration. For an earlier publication on the use of Post-it notes to influence behavior, see R. Garner (2005), "Post-it note persuasion: A sticky influence," *Journal of Consumer Psychology*, 15: pp. 230–237.

35. The Place Stinks: Smell and Association

For an overview of research into the influence of scent on behavior, see R. W. Holland, M. Hendriks, and H. Aarts (2005), "Smells like clean spirit: Nonconscious effects of scent on cognition and behavior," *Psychological Science*, 16: pp. 689–693. Their own research shows that lemon scents lead to cleaning jitters.

Scents leading to moral behavior are described in K. Liljenquist, C. B. Zhong, and A. D. Galinsky (2010), "The smell of virtue: Clean scents promote reciprocity and charity," *Psychological Science*, 21: pp. 381–383.

For Wen Li and colleagues' research showing that people in a room with a lemon scent are judged to be more pleasant, see W. Li, I. Moallem, K. A. Paller, and J. A. Gottfried (2007), "Subliminal smells can guide social preferences," *Psychological Science*, 18: pp. 1044–1049.

A study showing that women who smell of herbs are estimated to be five years younger is published as A. R. Hirsch and Y. Ye (2008), "Effects of odour on perception of age," *International Journal of Essential Oil Therapeutics*, 2(3): pp. 131–138.

Simone Schnall and colleagues have shown that people judge the behavior of others less harshly when in a fresh-smelling environment. Their research is published as S. Schnall, J. Benton, and S. Harvey (2008), "With a clean conscience: Cleanliness reduces the severity of moral judgments," *Psychological Science*, 19: pp. 1219–1222. For similar research see S. Schnall, J. Haidt, G. L. Clore, and A. H. Jordan (2008), "Disgust as embodied moral judgment," *Journal of Personality and Social Psychology*, 34: pp. 1096–1109.

Michael Kosfeld and colleagues have shown that investors who receive oxytocin nasal spray are much more reckless. See M. Kosfeld, M. Heinrichs, P. J. Zak, U. Fischbacher, and E. Fehr (2005), "Oxytocin increases trust in humans," *Nature*, 435: pp. 673–676.

36. Wealth is Damaging: Red Rags and Red Flags

For the study showing that a wealthy environment leads to unethical behavior, see F. Gino and L. Pierce (2009), "The abundance effect: Unethical behavior in the presence of wealth," *Organizational Behavior and Human Decision Processes*, 109: pp. 142–155. A similar effect is shown in research by Simone Moran and Maurice Schweitzer. The participants in their study were required to play a game in which those who were jealous of their opponent were more inclined to lie. See S. Moran and M. E. Schweitzer (2008), "When better is worse: Envy and the use of deception," *Negotiation and Conflict Management Research*, 1: pp. 3–29.

For the study by Kathleen Vohs and colleagues showing that the mere image of money leads to more selfish behavior, see K. D. Vohs, N. L. Mead, and M. R. Goode (2006), "The psychological consequences of money," *Science*, 314: pp. 1154–1156; K. D. Vohs, N. L. Mead, and M. R. Goode (2008), "Merely activating the concept of money changes personal and interpersonal behavior," *Current directions in Psychological Science*, 17: pp. 208–212.

37. Morals on Vacation: Cognitive Dissonance and Rationalizations

The theory of cognitive dissonance was first described in L. Festinger (1957), *A Theory of Cognitive Dissonance* (Evanston, IL: Row, Peterson).

For the study by Sykes and Matza in which five neutralization techniques are laid out, see G. M. Sykes and D. Matza (1957), "Techniques of neutralization: A theory of delinquency," *American Sociological Review*, 22: pp. 664–670.

For the research on chain smokers, see F. X. Gibbons, T. J. Eggleston, and A. C. Benthin (1997), "Cognitive reactions to smoking relapse: The reciprocal relation between dissonance and self-esteem," *Journal of Personality and Social Psychology*, 72: pp. 184–195.

For Festinger and Carlsmith's study showing the rationalizations used for speeding, see L. Festinger and J. M. Carlsmith (1959), "Cognitive consequences of forced compliance," *Journal of Abnormal and Social Psychology*, 58: pp. 203–210. Dissonance can occur even when no one else is involved and no damage or pain occurs. In Eddie Harmon-Jones and colleagues' experiment, the participants were required to drink an unpleasant-tasting drink. They were then asked to state voluntarily that it tasted good, something which they subsequently came to believe. This happened even if the participants were permitted to write down their opinion and immediately throw away the paper. See E. Harmon-Jones, J. W. Brehm, J. Greenberg, L. Simon, and D. E. Nelson (1996), "Evidence that the production of aversive consequences is not necessary to create cognitive dissonance," *Journal of Personality and Social Psychology*, 70: pp. 5–16. Dissonance can also arise from a decision taken in the past, if we later ask ourselves if we made the right choice. In order to suppress this effect we convince ourselves that we made the right choice. Robert Knox and James Inster researched this issue. In their experiment it turned out that people who have just bet on a horse race are much more certain that their horse will win than people still waiting in line to bet, although objectively the chances for each horse remain unchanged. This related to the irrevocability of the choice made. See R. E. Knox and J. A. Inster (1968), "Postdecision dissonance at post time," *Journal of Personality and Social Psychology*, 8: pp. 319–323.

For the study on arousing a sense of hypocrisy over water use in the sports complex, see C. A. Dickerson, R. Thibodeau, E. Aronson, and D. Miller (1992), "Using cognitive dissonance to encourage water conservation," *Journal of Applied Social Psychology*, 22: pp. 841–854.

Experimental research of Lisa Shu and her colleagues shows that people can engage in dishonest acts without feeling guilty about their behavior because they exhibit motivated forgetting of information that might otherwise limit their dishonesty. See L. L. Shu, F. Gino, and M. H. Bazerman (2011), "Dishonest deed, clear conscience: When cheating leads to moral disengagement and motivated forgetting," *Personality and Social Psychology Bulletin,* 37: pp. 330–349. In a later study, Shu and Gino demonstrate that those who cheat are more likely to forget the moral rules afterwards. See L. L. Shu and F. Gino (2012), "Sweeping dishonesty under the rug: How unethical actions lead to forgetting of moral rules," *Journal of Personality and Social Psychology*, 102: pp. 1164–1177.

38. The Mirror as a Reality Check: Objective Self-Awareness and Self-Evaluation

For the Halloween research into the effect of mirrors on theft of sweets, see A. L. Beaman, B. Klentz, E. Diener, and S. Svanum (1979), "Self-awareness and transgression in children: Two field studies," *Journal of Personality and Social Psychology*, 37: pp. 1835–1846.

There is a substantial body of literature on objective self-awareness. See, for example, S. Duval and R. Wickland (1972), *A Theory of Objective Self-Awareness* (New York: Academic Press); C. S. Carver and M. F. Scheier (1998), *On the Self-Regulation of Behavior* (New York: Cambridge University Press).

For the research into the relationship between long and short-term reflection and type of regret, see T. Gilovich and V. Husted Medvec (1995), "The experience of regret: What, when, and why," *Psychological Review*, 102: pp. 379–395.

Although looking into one's own eyes has positive effects, it could also help when people close their eyes and reflect on what is ethical or not. Research by Caruso and Gino demonstrate that people who consider situations with their eyes closed rather than open judge immoral behaviors as more unethical and moral behaviors as more ethical. See E. Caruso and F. Gino (2011), "Blind ethics: Closing one's eyes polarizes moral judgments and discourages dishonest behavior," *Cognition*, 2: pp. 280–285.

39. Constrained by the Eyes of Strangers: The Four Eyes Principle

Research showing that looking someone in the eye leads to greater compliance includes N. Guéguen and C. Jacob (2002), "Direct look versus evasive glance and compliance with a request," *Journal of Social Psychology*, 142:

pp. 393–396. For research showing that passers-by more readily take a leaflet if they are looked in the eye, see C. L. Kleinke and D. A. Singer (1979), "Influence of gaze on compliance with demanding and conciliatory requests in a field setting," *Personality and Social Psychology Bulletin*, 5: pp. 386–390. The effect of hitchhikers looking drivers in the eye is published in M. Snyder, J. Grether, and K. Keller (1974), "Staring and compliance: A field experiment on hitchhiking," *Journal of Applied Psychology*, 4: pp. 165–170.

For the study on the effect of posters showing eyes on people paying for coffee, see M. Bateson, D. Nettle, and G. Robert (2006), "Cues of being watched enhance cooperation in a real-world setting," *Biology Letters*, 2: pp. 412–414.

Further research into the four eyes principle includes J. M. Bering (2003), "On reading symbolic random events: Children's causal reasoning about unexpected occurrences," an article presented at the *Psychological and Cognitive Foundations of Religiosity Conference* in Atlanta; K. J. Haley and D. M. T. Fessler (2005), "Nobody's watching? Subtle cues affect generosity in an anonymous economic game," *Evolution and Human Behavior*, 26: pp. 245–256; J. M. Bering, K. McLeod, and T. K. Shackelford (2005), "Reasoning about dead agents reveals possible adaptive trends," *Human Nature*, 16: pp. 360–381; A. F. Shariff and A. Norenzayan (2007), "God is watching you: Priming God concepts increases prosocial behavior in an anonymous economic game," *Psychological Science*, 18: pp. 803–809.

In an experiment by Alejo Friere and colleagues it was shown that children as young as four pay attention to the eyes of another in an effort to discover the truth. In their experiment the lead researcher claimed not to know which of three upturned cups concealed a toy. Children under four took her at her word. Children of four saw that the lead researcher looked more toward one cup, which indeed turned out to conceal the toy. See A. Friere, M. Eskritt, and K. Lee (2004), "Are eyes windows to a deceiver's soul? Children's use of another's eye gaze cues in a deceptive situation," *Developmental Psychology*, 40: pp. 1093–1104.

40. Lamps and Sunglasses: Detection Theory, Controlitis, and the Spotlight Test

Donald Cressey's research among blue-collar criminals in prison is published as D. R. Cressey (1953), *Other People's Money: A Study in the Social Psychology of Embezzlement* (New York: Free Press).

For Henry Schneider's study of car repairs in Canada, see H. Schneider (2006), "A field experiment to measure agency problems in auto repair,"

Yale University research paper. Paul Tracy and James Fox's experiments also show that items covered by insurance are much more readily replaced at the garage. See P. E. Tracy and J. A. Fox (1989), "A field experiment on insurance fraud in auto body repair," *Criminology*, 27: pp. 589−603.

For the study on the effect of darkness and sunglasses on unethical behavior, see C. Zhong, V. Bohns, and F. Gino (2010), "Good lamps are the best police: Darkness increases dishonesty and self-interested behavior," *Psychological Science,* 21: pp. 311−314. Researchers also observed the effect of anonymity and deindividuation in the Halloween experiment described in Chapter 26. With masks, candy-stealing increased by two hundred and fifty percent. Just the idea that the children could not be recognized led them to steal more. See E. Diener, S. C. Fraser, A. L. Beaman, and R. T. Kelem (1976), "Effects of deindividuation variables on stealing among Halloween trick-or-treaters," *Journal of Personality and Social Psychology*, 33: pp. 178−183.

The phenomenon of "ironic processes of mental control" is described in D. M. Wegner, M. Ansfield, and D. Pilloff (1998), "The putt and the pendulum: Ironic effects of the mental control of action," *Psychological Science*, 9: pp. 196−199.

It appears that people behave differently if others can see what they are up to. Research shows that 90 percent of students washed their hands if another person was present when they went to the toilet, whereas when no one else was present the figure was less than 20 percent. At the same time the so-called floodlight effect can lead to people thinking that others see more than they actually see. This effect was researched by Tom Gilovich and colleagues. The participants were required to wear a garishly offensive t-shirt in the company of others. The subjects thought on average that 46 percent of those present had noticed their t-shirt, when in fact only 23 percent had noticed. See T. Gilovich, V. Husted Medvec, and K. Savitsky (2000), "The spotlight effect in social judgment: An egocentric bias in estimates of the salience of one's own actions and appearance," *Journal of Personality and Social Psychology*, 78: pp. 211−222; T. Gilovich, J. Kruger, and V. Husted Medvec (2002), "The spotlight effect revisited: Overestimating the manifest variability of our actions and appearance," *Journal of Experimental Social Psychology*, 38: pp. 93−99.

41. Deceptive Appearances: Moral Self-Fulfillment and the Compensation Effect

For Nina Mazar and Chen-Bo Zhong's research on consumers lying and stealing more after buying sustainable products, see N. Mazar and C. Zhong (2010), "Do green products make us better people?" *Psychological Science*, 21: pp. 494−498.

Recent research described by Richard Wiseman in his book *Quirkology* (2007) shows that more than 50 percent of the western population believe that clean-shaven men are more honest than men with beards.

For John Stewart's research showing that good-looking men receive lighter punishments for the same crimes, see J. E Stewart, II (1980), "Defendants' attractiveness as a factor in the outcome of trials," *Journal of Applied Social Psychology*, 10: pp. 348–361.

For a meta-analysis of research into people's inability to tell from a person's exterior whether they are lying, see C. F. Bond, Jr. and B. M. DePaulo (2008), "Individual differences in judging deception: Accuracy and bias," *Psychological Bulletin*, 134: pp. 477–492.

For the study on the time taken over lying, see A. P. Gregg (2007), "When vying reveals lying: The timed antagonistic response alethiometer," *Applied Cognitive Psychology*, 21: pp. 621–647.

For research showing that cheats are remembered longer, see L. Mealy, C. Daood, and M. Krage (1996), "Enhanced memory for faces of cheating," *Ethology and Sociobiology*, 17: pp. 119–128; D. Chiappe and A. Brown (2004), "Cheaters are looked at longer and remembered better than cooperators in social exchange situations," *Evolutionary Psychology*, 2: pp. 108–120.

42. Perverse Effects of Transparency: Moral Licensing and the Magnetic Middle

For research on the perverse effects of publicizing conflicts of interest, see D. M. Cain, G. Loewenstein, and D. A. Moore (2005), "The dirt on coming clean: Perverse effects of disclosing conflicts of interest," *Journal of Legal Studies*, 34: pp. 1–25.

For Wesley Schultz and colleagues' research on the effect of social norms on energy use, see P. W. Schultz, J. M. Nolan, R. B. Cialdini, N. J. Goldstein, and V. Griskevicius (2007), "The constructive, destructive, and reconstructive power of social norms," *Psychological Science*, 18: pp. 429–434. Transparency over salaries also tends to drive them up rather than down. In my inaugural lecture, *De Open Onderneming* (The Open Enterprise, 2003), I pointed to a number of moral risks and limits of transparency.

43. A Problem Shared is a Problem Halved: Communication Theory

For research on the effect of discussion groups on dietary change, see K. Lewin (1947), "Group decision and social change," in T. M. Newcomb and E. L. Hartley (Eds.), *Readings in Social Psychology* (New York: Holt): pp. 330–344.

Communication theory has been explained among others by R. T. Craig (1999), "Communication theory as a field," *Communication Theory*, 9: pp. 161–199. Mieneke Weenig and Cees Midden show that when it comes to energy saving people are motivated by social interaction in their neighborhood. See M. W. H. Weenig and C. J. H. Midden (1991), "Communication network influences on information diffusion and persuasion," *Journal of Personality and Social Psychology*, 61: pp. 734–742. Other research shows that instructions from peers are more effective than instructions from superiors. Luepker and colleagues have demonstrated this in reducing smoking. See R. V. Luepker, C. A. Johnson, D. M. Murray, and T. F. Pechacek (1983), "Prevention of cigarette smoking: Three-year follow-up of an education program for youth," *Journal of Behavioral Medicine*, 6: pp. 53–62.

For the study by Charles Lord and colleagues showing that people who are forced to consider a different way of seeing things make better decisions, see C. G. Lord, M. R. Lepper, and E. Preston (1984), "Considering the opposite: A corrective strategy for social judgment," *Journal of Personality and Social Psychology*, 47: pp. 1231–1243.

For research showing that a simple question can lead to different behavior, see A. G. Greenwald, C. G. Carnot, R. Beach, and B. Young (1987), "Increasing voting behavior by asking people if they expect to vote," *Journal of Applied Psychology*, 72: pp. 315–318; V. G. Morwitz, E. Johnson, and D. Schmittlein (1993), "Does measuring intent change behavior?" *Journal of Consumer Research*, 20: pp. 46–61; J. Levav and G. J. Fitzsimons (2006), "When questions change behavior," *Psychological Science*, 17: pp. 207–213.

Many experiments show that participation in decision making leads to more commitment and enjoyment in implementing decisions, even when this relates to difficult activities or really horrible tasks, such as eating worms. See, for example, I. Janis and L. Mann (1977), *Decision Making* (New York: Free Press).

44. What You See Is Not What You Say: Group Pressure and Conformity

For Solomon Asch's experiment, see S. E. Asch (1955), "Opinions and social pressure," *Scientific American*, 193(5): pp. 31–35. Stanley Milgram's experiment (Chapter 18) related to obedience to authority, whereas Ach's experiment was about conformity with peers.

Rob Bond conducted a meta-analysis of 125 studies on the relationship between group size and conformity. See R. Bond (2005), "Group size and conformity," *Group Processes & Intergroup Relations*, 8(4): pp. 331–354.

For follow-up research into the effect of one dissident on conformity, see V. L. Allen and J. M. Levine (1971), "Social support and conformity: The role of independent assessment of reality," *Journal of Experimental Social Psychology*, 7: pp. 48−58.

45. Explaining, Speaking Out, and Letting Off Steam: Pressure Build-Up under Thought Suppression

Jerald Greenberg's research on the effect of communication on theft was published as J. Greenberg (1990), "Employee theft as a reaction to under-payment inequity: The hidden costs of pay cuts," *Journal of Applied Psychology*, 75: pp. 561−568.

For research into the health risks of thought suppression, see K. J. Petri, R. J. Booth, and J. W. Pennebaker (1998), "The immunological effects of thought suppression," *Journal of Personality and Social Psychology*, 75: pp. 1264−1272. Not thinking about something also takes energy. See for example R. Occhipinti, E. Somersalo, and D. Calvetti (2010), "Energetics of inhibition: Insights with a computational model of the human >gabaergic neuron−astrocyte cellular complex," *Journal of Cerebral Blood Flow & Metabolism*, 30: pp. 1834−1846.

46. Blow the Whistle and Sound the Alarm: The Bystander Effect and Pluralistic Ignorance

For the study by John Darley and Bibb Latané on the bystander effect, see J. M. Darley and B. Latané (1968), "Bystander intervention in emergencies: Diffusion of responsibility," *Journal of Personality and Social Psychology*, 8: pp. 377−383; B. Latané and J. M. Darley (1970), *The Unresponsive Bystander: Why Doesn't He Help?* (Englewood Cliffs: Prentice Hall). The verbatim text of the person who was taken ill during the experiment was, "I-er-um-I think I-I need-er-if-if could-er-er-somebody er-er-er-er-er-er-er give me a little-er-give me a little help here because-er-I-er-I'm-er-erh-h-having a-a-a real problem-er-right now and I-er-if somebody could help me out it would-it would-er-er s-s-sure be-sure be good ... because-there-er-er-a cause I-er-I-uh-I've got a-a one of the-er-sei er-er-things coming on and-and-and I could really-er-use some help so if somebody would-er-give me a little h-help-uh-er-er-er-er-er c-could somebody-er-er-help-er-uh-uh-uh [accompanied by choking sounds] ... I'm gonna die-er-er-I'm ... gonna die-er-help-er-er-seizure-er- [another choking sound and then silence]."

The reasons for bystander apathy discussed in this chapter also feature in the review article B. Latané and S. Nida (1981), "Ten years of research on group size and helping," *Psychological Bulletin*, 89: pp. 308–324.

A substantial body of other research has been conducted on bystander apathy, varying from smoke in a waiting room, people dropping things and finding objects in the street. See, for example, R. Wiseman (2007), *Quirkology: The curious science of everyday lives*, (London: Pan Macmillan). The studies show that the more cities grow the less people help one another. Explanations for this include the overload of information in larger cities, anonymity and loneliness, and the faster pace of life. An interesting question is whether this also applies to organizations: does bystander apathy increase the bigger an organization is?

Pluralistic ignorance can also relate to the behavior of others and their social norms. Research shows that students overestimate the alcohol intake of their peers, which in turn affects their own behavior. See D. A. Prentice and D. T. Miller (1993), "Pluralistic ignorance and alcohol use on campus: Some consequences of misperceiving the social norm," *Journal of Personality and Social Psychology*, 64: pp. 243–256.

47. The Value of Appreciation: Compliments and the Midas Effect

For research showing that the more ethical behavior is rewarded the more ethically managers and employees behave, see S. Román and J. L. Munuera (2005), "Determinants and consequences of ethical behavior: An empirical study of salespeople," *European Journal of Marketing*, 39: pp. 473–495.

For research into the effects of showing appreciation for donations to good causes, see R. E. Kraut (1973), "Effects of social labeling on giving to charity," *Journal of Experimental Social Psychology*, 9: pp. 551–562.

For research showing the effects compliments have on the tips hairdressers receive, see A. H. Crusco and C. G. Wetzel (1984), "The Midas touch: The effects of interpersonal touch on restaurant tipping," *Personality and Social Psychology Bulletin*, 10: pp. 512–517. See also J. S. Seiter and E. Dutson (2007), "The effect of compliments on tipping behavior in hairstyling salons," *Journal of Applied Social Psychology*, 37: pp. 1999–2007. Research shows that words of thanks increase self-motivation and self-esteem, leading to more prosocial behavior. See A. M. Grant and F. Gino (2010), "A little thanks goes a long way: Explaining why gratitude expressions motivate prosocial behavior," *Journal of Personality and Social Psychology*, 98: pp. 946–955.

Research showing that physical contact leads to a greater appetite for risk was carried out by Jonathan Levav and Jennifer Argo of Columbia University. See J. Levav and J. J. Argo (2010), "Physical contact and financial risk-taking," *Psychological Science*, 21: pp. 804–810. The cause may be a feeling of security developed in youth in association with parental touch. Mothers might give their sons confidence for risky undertakings, such as first steps or a first bicycle ride with a pat on the shoulder. In later life that can lead to a misplaced sense of security when making financial decisions under the influence of a feminine touch.

48. Washing Dirty Hands: Self-Absolution and the Macbeth Effect

Chen-Bo Zhong and Katie Liljenquist's research into the Macbeth effect is published in C. B. Zhong and K. Liljenquist (2006), "Washing away your sins: Threatened morality and physical cleansing," *Science*, 313: pp. 145–146.

Research by Spike Lee and Norbert Schwartz shows that people who wash their hands after a difficult decision are less troubled by doubts afterwards. Cleaning the hands makes people feel that they can literally wash away their worries. See S. W. S. Lee and N. Schwarz (2006), "Washing away postdecisional dissonance," *Science*, 328: p. 709.

49. Punishment Pitfalls: Deterrence Theory

On biases in judging transgressors and transgressions, see K. J. Dunegan (1996), "Fines, frames, and images: Examining formulation effects on punishment decisions," *Organizational Behavior and Human Decision Processes*, 68: pp. 58–67; Chapters 11–15 of the 2007 book *Irrationality* by Stuart Sutherland (London: Pinter & Martin).

Deborah Small and George Loewenstein show that people are harsher in their judgments of transgressors they know less well. See D. A. Small and G. Loewenstein (2005), "The devil you know: The effect of identifiability on punitiveness," *Journal of Behavioral Decision Making*, 18: pp. 311–318.

For research showing that the death penalty increases murder figures, see W. C. Baily and R. D. Peterson (1997), "Murder, capital punishment, and deterrence: A review of literature," in H. A. Bedau (Ed.), *The Death Penalty in America: Current Controversies* (New York: Oxford University Press): pp. 135–161; A. Sakamoto, K. Sekiguchi, and A. Shinkyu (2003), "Does media coverage of capital punishment have a deterrent effect on the occurrence of brutal crimes? An analysis of Japanese time-series data from 1959 to 1990," in K. Yang, K. Hwang, P. B. Pedersen, and I. Daibo (Eds.), *Progress in Asian social psychology: Conceptual and empirical contributions* (Westport: Preager): pp. 277–290. Marray Straus and colleagues' research, as presented at the *International Conference on Violence, Abuse and Trauma* in San Diego, shows that a corrective smack makes children less intelligent.

For research on the second punishment pitfall, that trust is further reduced when a previously introduced system of sanctions is removed, see D. de Cremer (Ed.) (2009), *Psychological Perspectives on Ethical Behavior and Decision Making* (Greenwich: Information Age Publishing).

With respect to the third pitfall, that more severe punishments lead to greater tolerance for transgressions, see D. Kahan (2000), "Gentle nudges vs. hard shoves: Solving the sticky norms problem," *The University of Chicago Law Review*, 67: pp. 607–643.

In order to avoid too severe a punishment, one might use Seiji Takaku's research in which a feeling of hypocrisy was aroused. Takaku researched road rage. The subjects were required to take part in a simulation in which one party unintentionally cut in front of another. This group reacted much less aggressively when they themselves were cut off. In being aware of their own behavior, people also see the behavior of others differently. In order to avoid severe punishments, it can therefore be a good idea to examine one's own behavior. See S. Takaku (2006), "Reducing road rage: An application of the dissonance-attribution model of interpersonal forgiveness," *Journal of Applied Social Psychology*, 36: pp. 2362–2378.

For Elliot Aronson and Merrill Carlsmith's study showing mild punishments to be more effective in changing behavior than severe punishments, see A. Elliot and J. M. Carlsmith (1963), "Effect of the severity of threat on the devaluation of forbidden behavior," *Journal of Abnormal and Social Psychology*, 66: pp. 584–588.

50. The Price of a Penalty: The Crowding-Out Effect

For Uri Gneezy and Aldo Rustichini's research into the effects of penalties at nurseries, see U. Gneezy and A. Rustichini (2000), "A fine is a price," *Journal of Legal Studies*, 29: pp. 1–17.

51. The Corrupting Influence of Rewards and Bonuses: The Overjustification Effect

For the study by David Greene and colleagues on how extrinsic motives can displace intrinsic motives, see D. Greene, B. Sternberg, and M. R.

Lepper (1976), "Overjustification in a token economy," *Journal of Personality and Social Psychology*, 34: pp. 1219–1234. For a similar study, see M. R. Lepper, D. Greene, and R. E. Nisbett (1973), "Undermining children's intrinsic interest with extrinsic rewards: A test of the 'overjustification' hypothesis," *Journal of Personal and Social Psychology*, 28: pp. 129–137.

For several studies showing that financial rewards displace intrinsic motives, see B. S. Frey and F. Oberholzer-Gee (1997), "The cost of price incentives: An empirical analysis of motivation crowding-out," *American Economic Review*, 87: pp. 746–755; A. A. Stukas, M. Snyder, and E. G. Clary (1999), "The effects of 'mandatory volunteerism' on intentions to volunteer," *Psychological Science*, 10: pp. 59–64; R. Titmuss (1971), "The gift of blood," *Transaction*, 8(3): pp. 18–26. For a meta-analysis of experiments on the effect of extrinsic rewards on intrinsic motivation, see E. L. Deci, R. Koestner, and R. M. Ryan (1999), "A meta-analytic review of experiments examining the effects of extrinsic rewards on intrinsic motivation," *Psychological Bulletin*, 125: pp. 627–668.

52. The Heinz Dilemma: Levels of Moral Development

Lawrence Kohlberg's model of moral development is described in L. Kohlberg (1981), *Essays on Moral Development, Vol. I: The Philosophy of Moral Development* (San Francisco: Harper & Row). According to Rest and colleagues less than 20 percent of Americans reach the third level. See J. Rest, D. Narvaez, M. Bebeau, and S. Thoma (1999), "A Neo-Kohlbergian approach: The DIT and schema theory," *Educational Psychology Review*, 11: pp. 291–324. The model has also been criticized by Carol Gilligan, among others, in her 1982 book, *In a Different Voice* (Cambridge: Harvard University Press).

James Weber and David Wasieleski show that people argue at a lower level at work than in private situations. See J. Weber (1990), "Managers' moral reasoning: Assessing their responses to three moral dilemmas," *Human Relations*, 43: pp. 687–702; J. Weber and D. Wasieleski (2001), "Investigating influences on managers' moral reasoning: The impact of context, personal, and organizational factors," *Business and Society*, 40: pp. 79–111.

About the Author

Muel Kaptein has worked as an academic and consultant in business ethics since 1991. In his current position as partner at KPMG, together with colleagues, he supports organizations in investigating and improving their integrity, soft controls, fraud risk management, compliance, and sustainability.

He is also a professor of business ethics and integrity management at the Erasmus University of Rotterdam. His research focuses on areas such as measuring and managing integrity in organizations, and he teaches courses in leadership, sustainability, and governance.

He has published more than 40 articles in international scientific journals such as *Academy of Management Review*, *Human Relations*, *Journal of Organizational Behavior* and *Journal of Management*. He is a coeditor of the *Journal of Business Ethics*. He is an author and coauthor of various books including *Ethics Management* (Springer, 1998), *The Balanced Company* (Oxford University Press, 2002), *The Six Principles for Managing with Integrity* (Articulate Press, 2005), and *The Living Code* (Greenleaf, 2008).

He is married and has five children.

Printed in the United States
By Bookmasters